FABULOUS FLOWERBEDS
Inspiration • Planting • Care

HORTICULTURE
BOOKS
CINCINNATI, OHIO

FABULOUS FLOWERBEDS

Inspiration · Planting · Care

Gisela Keil / Jürgen Becker

A DAVID & CHARLES BOOK

David & Charles is a subsidiary of F+W (UK) Ltd., an F+W Publications Inc. company

First published in the US in 2004 ISBN 1-55870-733-6 paperback

Originally published under the title *Die Kunst der Beete*
© 2003 by Deutsche Verlags-Anstalt GmbH, Stuttgart München

Distributed in North America by Horticulture Books, an imprint of F+W Publications, Inc.
4700 East Galbraith Road, Cincinnati, OH 45236
1-800-289-0963

Printed in China by SNP Leefung
for David & Charles
Brunel House   Newton Abbot   Devon

Desk Editor: Sarah Martin
Production Controller: Roger Lane

Visit our website at www.davidandcharles.co.uk

David & Charles books are available from all good bookshops; alternatively you can contact
our Orderline on (0)1626 334555 or write to us at FREEPOST EX2110, David & Charles Direct,
Newton Abbot, TQ12 4ZZ (no stamp required UK mainland).

Contents

FLOWERBEDS: POSITION, FUNCTION, STYLE

Site and Aspect

In almost any garden setting, flowerbeds play an essential role. With creativity and imagination, flowers, shrubs, ornamental and edible plants are brought into play, lending a sense of style to any design. Flowerbeds set the mood of the garden: flanking paths (above), fences and walls with stunning borders; adding colourful splendour and heavenly fragrances to patios and seating areas (left-hand page); or blending in with shady areas, under trees or beside a pond to create an idyllic scene. However you decide to use them, flowerbeds are guaranteed to give the garden a truly individual character.

Following and Edging Paths

Flowers and flowering plants are a wonderful gift from nature and all who delight in them long to be able to see more of their colours and enjoy their beautiful fragrances, and one of the best ways to do this in your garden is to plant them in flowerbeds that are positioned beside paths.

Such beds can also create strong garden designs. The horizontal outline they produce provides structure, while the plants they contain offer colour and shape and three-dimensionality. Combining the right plants from the wide range now available will supply you with fantastic sensual experiences that change with the seasons.

When considering the size, style and colour of flowerbeds to follow and border paths, always keep in mind the surface and course of the path. It is only when both path and flowerbed are in harmony that the final design objective can be achieved, be it an imposing boulevard or a secluded footpath.

Linking paths and flowerbeds

Flowerbeds and paths can be combined in a wide variety of ways:

▷ Flowerbeds can be used to flank both sides or just one side of a straight or winding path. In formal gardens, they can be laid out in symmetrical shapes, whereas in informal gardens they can be more irregular.

▷ Flowerbeds can also be used in varying widths as an attractive border to follow the

Left-hand page top: *Formal flowerbeds contained by box (*Buxus sempervirens) *and planted with low flowers and long-stemmed roses to add height.*

Left-hand page bottom: *These flowerbeds provide a natural carpet underneath the trees.*

Right: *Specimen shaped box adds height and interest, standing out among lower-growing plants in the flowerbeds.*

course of the path. They can be arranged in a single or double line, perhaps giving precedence to small and delicately flowered plants that do not make a bold statement but nevertheless lend an intimate character that can be enjoyed from the close proximity of a path.

▷ Next to entrances, in the front garden or beside a fence, flowerbeds play a more prestigious role and thus require architectural or more colourful flowering plants to create a stronger impact when viewed from a distance.

▷ A variety of interesting effects can be achieved by matching the size of the paths and flowerbeds. When they are on both sides of a path, narrow flowerbeds with plants in muted colours play a subordinate role and emphasize the course of the path and its surface. Carefully shaped box edges are also suitable for creating this effect. Wide flowerbeds, in contrast, deflect the focus away from the path, especially when the plants at the edge of the flowerbeds are allowed to encroach on to the path itself.

This mixed double border is resplendent in early and mid-summer with its cool colours. Its creator shows the subtlety and sensitivity of a painter through her use of colours and shapes, creating wonderful compositions with different groups of plants: herbaceous perennials such as delphiniums and herbs such as purple sage. Topiary box and yew help to stabilize the composition.

Making the most of height

By keeping a bordering flowerbed at a low level, like a carpet, you can create a light and spacious area. Borders of flowers are often planted in kitchen gardens to provide some extra colour. Using low-growers will ensure that the vegetables behind are not overshadowed. The Victorians were fond of carpet-bedding, planting flowerbeds with low-growing plants in a variety of colours. However, when they are large, flowerbeds of this kind can be rather monotonous and are best broken up with vertical structures. Long-stemmed plants, tall herbaceous perennials and shrubs or climbing

plants trailed over an obelisk will add height to the bed. As long as these vertical features are narrow, with small crowns, there will still be enough light underneath for annuals and herbaceous perennials.

In contrast, classical borders gradually ascend from the path to the back of the garden and are often bordered by walls, clipped hedges or loosely arranged shrubs. If they rise steeply on both sides of the path, they will give the impression of a gorge-like corridor, drawing attention to the imposing planting as you walk along the path. Another alternative is a one-sided border, leaving the path or lawn open to the front, setting off the boundary of the garden – or part of the garden – as a finishing touch. Classical herbaceous borders need plenty of sunshine and will look beautiful when they are filled with attractive combinations of flowering perennials complemented by decorative leafy plants. Their different flowering periods will ensure either constant or changing colour, depending on the choice of plants.

With a longer flowering time than the classical herbaceous border, the mixed border includes perennials and grasses as well as early-blooming bulbs, summer flowers, roses and shrubs. Evergreen shrubs such as box provide lasting structure while any gaps can be filled with beautiful annuals.

Borders can also be created in shady or partially shaded areas. Although flowers will not be so abundant here, shrubs and many herbaceous perennials can have impressive foliage. Even borders planted exclusively with shrubs can be very attractive; for example a path under tall trees lined with rhododendrons, azaleas and conifers looks wonderful, especially in spring.

Tips: Practical borders

▷ In order to present their magical charm to the full, borders should be at least 2m (6ft 6in) wide and 5m (16ft) long.

▷ When designing wide borders, make sure they are accessible by paths or stepping stones for planting.

▷ The more variety in the border, the calmer the framing pathway should be. Grass is ideal.

Top: *Autumn borders with a few judiciously placed shrubs set the tone with their rhythmic repetition; reed grass* (Achnatherum brachytricha) *and hemp agrimony* (Eupatorium) *play a leading role.*

Above: *A wide border engulfs a bench in a swirling sea of flowers.*

By Patios and Seating Areas

Flowerbeds next to open seating areas need to satisfy our primeval need for protection from behind as well as taking into account our need for privacy. They should also indulge our desire for beautiful landscaping, colourful plants and floral fragrances.

Practical considerations

A house bordering the patio will already ensure a good level of security. If you are planning an open seating area, however, you will need to draw up a list of basic requirements. A flowerbed with shrubs, roses, tall herbaceous perennials and grasses, a clipped hedge, and the leafy canopy of a tree or a trellis with climbing flowers, will provide natural protection from behind, above or to the sides.

Wherever the patio or seating area is sited, there should be flowerbeds close by. This will enable the plants and their different fragrances to transport us to another, more peaceful, world where we can relax and recover from the stresses of everyday life. Birds will be attracted to the garden and we can sit back and watch them and the plants from a perfect vantage point. When planning a flowerbed beside a patio, the gardener needs to decide whether the seating area is to be enclosed at the front or half-encircled and where the access point will be. You could create access through the flowerbed or to the sides. The alternative is to have two flowerbeds on on either side of the patio, the centre being open and so allowing good access to the garden.

This early summer display created by iris (Iris germanica), columbine (Aquilegia) and tree lupin (Lupinus arboreus) proves that flowerbeds can enrich open seating areas. They also interlink benches or groups of seats within the garden, integrating them into the composition as a whole.

Transitional designs

Patio flowerbeds form the meeting point between the garden and the house. It is best to prevent an abrupt transition from the structural to the floral world by avoiding harsh breaks. Patio surfaces can be arranged to spill over into the flowerbed in sloping, staggered or sweeping patterns. Most patios, however, are still laid in a rectangular formation. Linear transitions can be disguised by planting up to the edge of the flowerbed and letting the flowers grow on to the patio.

Patios appear especially romantic when the green of the garden continues right up to the house, for example by allowing climbing plants to grow up the sides of the building. Climbing roses, clematis or vines can be planted in patio flowerbeds and will soon cover a trellis, giving privacy or protection from the wind. They may also spread to the house itself. Alternatively, they can be planted beside a house wall or left to climb up over the posts of a pergola fixed in the flowerbed. Climbing shrubs are often rather sparse at their base, so attractive summer plants such as lavender or irises can be planted to disguise this.

Planting tips

Patio flowerbeds must be designed with great care because they are constantly visible all year round. They should therefore be pleasing to look at throughout the seasons. In spring, this can be accomplished with bulb flowers; from summer to

Top: A wild and shady flowerbed is decked out with ferns, plantain lilies (Hosta) and yellow corydalis (Corydalis lutea) under the green canopy of a leafy tree.
Above: The sunny location of this patio is ideal for a fragrant flowerbed, whose flowers and pleasant perfumes charmingly complement the climbing rose 'New Dawn' on the nearby house wall. Delicate flowers are best enjoyed close up, making them the perfect patio partner.

autumn with annuals and herbaceous perennials; while evergreen shrubs and ivy are highly decorative all year round. The following criteria should be considered:

▷ Fragrance: herbs and scented plants enchant both day and night with their sweet fragrances.

▷ Colours: choose harmonious colours. Be careful not to jar the eye; avoid the use of gaudy contrasts or a riotous profusion of colour.

▷ Height: choose mainly low-growing plants to avoid blocking the view into the garden.

▷ Attractive features: include one or two tall or eyecatching features, for example ornamental shrubs, roses, tall ornamental grasses, climbing plants on an obelisk or annuals arranged in a charming bowl on top of a column or high up in an amphora.

▷ Privacy: if you have a sloping patio, avoid feeling like you are on show, by surrounding the area with tall shrubs or pergolas covered in greenery. These should, however, be arranged and planted so that the view is kept free. Gentle embankments can be planted directly. Make the most of steep slopes by laying terraces of horizontal flowerbeds, ensuring access to the garden with paths and steps.

Planting blue catmint (Nepeta x faassenii) and pink cranesbill (Geranium endressii) in the foreground hides the bare bases of the climbing roses and tall shrubs in this patio flowerbed.

Lightweight garden furniture can be moved to be near each of your garden's highlights. Here, a central lawn enables the owner to put seats near overflowing flowerbeds, allowing them to sit and enjoy the spicy herbal fragrances of Santolina rosmarinifolia, thyme, oregano, lesser calamint (Calamintha nepeta) and silvery bunches of curry plant (Helichrysum italicum). Their subtle colouring complements the carmine red of sedum 'Ruby Glow'.

Shaded by Shrubs and Walls

Deep shadow can be found under shrubs and also in small gardens and inner courtyards surrounded by high walls or houses. Flowerbeds at the foot of tall hedges are often partially shaded, depending on their location, but that also means that they receive some sun during the course of the day. Whether in deep or partial shade, attractive arrangements of plants can be incorporated into the design. A wide range of shade-loving or shade-tolerant shrubs and climbing plants as well as perennials are available for such areas. Some particularly good results can be achieved using perennials and shrubs that have large and highly decorative leaves, although it should be borne in mind that the large leaves may be compensating for the plant having comparatively small flowers.

Shady beds in front of walls

Borders can also be arranged on the shady side of walls. To prevent the walls themselves from looking too out of place in the garden, they could be partially covered with shade-loving climbers such as common ivy (*Hedera helix*), climbing hydrangea (*Hydrangea anomala* ssp. *petiolaris*), honeysuckle (*Lonicera*) or with varieties of *Clematis montana* or *C. viticella*. All these will flourish at the shady base of the wall and climb upwards to receive the light they require. Shrubs can also form a link between flowerbeds and walls, especially evergreens such as yew (*Taxus*), mountain laurel (*Kalmia latifolia*) and lily-of-the-valley bush (*Pieris japonica*).

If flowerbeds reach right up to the building, take care to avoid covering the damp-proof course. If you are concerned about the brickwork use a waterproof coating. For plants, these areas are problematical if overhanging roofing prevents them from receiving any rain or if building rubble has been left behind.

As most shady plants like slightly moist soil with humus, remove any deeply buried building rubble and then enrich the ground with well-rotted manure or garden compost to provide humus, or even replace the soil. After planting, the humus layer can be built up with regular mulching and watering, ensuring the required level of moisture. William Robinson (1838–1935), who has been described as 'one of the greatest gardeners of all time', advised combining herbaceous perennials with evergreen flowering shrubs to maintain their attraction even in the winter; this is a sensible idea, particularly in this type of site.

Shady beds in front of and under shrubs

Shady flowerbeds can give an air of romance when lining a path through a wild garden shaded with tall shrubs but they are usually placed under or in front of individual trees or shrubs, groups of woody plants or hedges to create artistic garden compositions. This effect is only achieved, however, when the plants are compatible and complement each other visually.

▷ Birch trees, maples, beech trees, alders, poplars, ornamental cherry trees and robinias have such dense roots that they can crowd out many

Left-hand page top: *This shady border makes clever use of the different shades of green provided by the plantain lilies* (Hosta), *supported by the climbing hydrangea on the wall.*
Left-hand page bottom: *Shrubs such as box and hydrangea can be placed under other plants and require very little room for their roots. Box is pleasing to the eye even in winter with its structure and colour and hydrangea lightens up the area in summer.*
Top: *Formal circular planting with pink cranesbill* (Geranium endressii).
Above: *Natural combinations with plantain lilies* (Hosta), *violet-blue purple cranesbill* (Geranium x magnificum) *and lady's mantle* (Alchemilla mollis).

shade-loving shrubs and bedding plants or compete too fiercely with them for water and minerals.

▷ Other trees such as horse chestnut, elder and walnut store quantities of tannin in their leaves; when the leaves fall, these make their way into the soil and act as a growth inhibitor.

▷ Trees and shrubs that have a tendency to produce runners are only suitable for having herbaceous perennials planted near them if they have been surrounded by root barriers, preventing them from growing into the flowerbeds. These include ornamental cherries (*Prunus*), stag's horn sumach (*Rhus typhina*), mountain ash (*Sorbus aucuparia*) and red-barked dogwood (*Cornus alba*).

Planting tips

Spring begins under leafy shrubs with the delicate floral blooms of small bulb flowers such as snowdrops, daffodils, winter aconites and windflowers, which flourish under the protection and humus provided by the fallen leaves. As the bulbs quickly take root they can be placed between groundcover plants which then take over to form the summer display; groundcover plants are undemanding and quickly provide lasting greenery, for example common ivy (*Hedera helix*), Japanese spurge (*Pachysandra terminalis*) or small evergreens such as periwinkle (*Vinca minor*). To increase the herbaceous perennials' chances, it is best to plant them at the same time as the shrubs. Under older, deeply rooted trees it often helps to use soil banks for the underplanting. Many shrubs, however, do not tolerate this very well.

*Bush roses in front of this patio's rose-covered pergola: in the gentle shade of a pear tree, together they exude their warm summer fragrances along with lavender and cranesbill (*Geranium sanguineum *var.* striatum) in a free arrangement.*

By Water

Top: *The large rounded shield-like leaves of the Japanese sweet coltsfoot (Petasites japonicus) contrast with the narrow spears of the bulrush (Typha latifolia).*
Above: *The umbrella plant (Darmera peltata) creates a sensational scene twice a year; in spring with its leafless pink-coloured flower umbels, and in autumn with its magnificently coloured leaves which grow up to 60cm (24in) in width.*

Water can enhance areas with a bustling torrent or a calm stillness in both natural and formal gardens, creating the impression of another world. Flowing or cascading water will bring a lively character to the garden. Pools and ponds, on the other hand, create an air of meditative tranquillity, mirroring the sky and the surrounding nature.

Flowerbeds beside formal water features

Raised or ground-level ornamental pools in a variety of geometric shapes are the most common types of water feature used in both classical and modern formal gardens. Nearly always featuring a clearly outlined structure, they have a mainly decorative and aesthetic function and often only need a sparse surrounding of plants. Plants in bordering decorative flowerbeds or containers will also add allure to the pool area. Annuals, herbaceous perennials and shrubs are all suitable for siting near formal water features, provided the soil they are in is well-drained.

Flowerbeds beside natural ponds and brooks

The diversity of nature provides the perfect model for planting beside informal ponds. The banks of marshy, still water areas should be lined with plants that will tolerate being partially submerged if the water level rises appreciably. So-called marginal herbaceous perennials can be used to provide an impressive and dense frame from behind. To create a really authentic natural layout,

Decorative shrubs by a natural pond

▷ Japanese maple (*Acer japonicum, A. palmatum*)

▷ Flowering dogwood (*Cornus florida, C. kousa*)

▷ Snowball tree (*Viburnum opulus, V. plicatum* f. *tomentosum* 'Mariesii')

▷ Rhododendron species and hybrids

▷ Hortensia (*Hydrangea* species and varieties)

▷ Willow (*Salix* species and varieties)

▷ Snowy mespilus (*Amelanchier lamarckii*)

provide only a narrow path to allow maintenance and access to a seating area near the pond. Flowerbeds can be very free and lush in this transitional area between water and land with a varied selection of flowers, leaf structures and plant forms. Tall grasses and attractive solitary shrubs are indispensable highlights; plant them a slight distance from the pond so that their falling leaves do not disturb the water.

Set against the red autumn colouring of the loosestrife (Lysimachia clethroides) on the banks of the river, silver grass (Miscanthus species) and moor grass (Molinia species) are both truly dazzling, with their golden red fountain-like stems.

Natural ponds with smooth inclining banks are the perfect setting for marsh and marginal herbaceous perennials, creating a seamless transition between garden and pond. While bulrush (Typha latifolia), *the graceful grass-like flowering rush* (Butomus umbellatus) and *sweet flag* (Acorus calamus 'Variegatus') *merrily splash about in the still water area, the tri-coloured planting on the bank is seen in all its glory. The yellow colour theme starts at the edge of the water with ligularia* (Ligularia veitchiana, L. przewalskii), *continues in the foreground with a field of pot marigolds* (Calendula officinalis 'Lemon Beauty'), *progresses into a few nettle-leaved mulleins* (Verbascum chaixii) *and culminates in fragrant yellow balls of common meadow rue* (Thalictrum flavum ssp. glaucum). Hound's tongue (Cynoglossum nervosum) *and anise hyssop* (Agastache foeniculum) *mixed in between add dabs of light blue while meadowsweet* (Filipendula purpurea f. albiflora), *goat's rue* (Galega officinalis 'Alba') *and loosestrife* (Lysimachia clethroides) *provide a shower of summery white.*

On a Slope

Gardens situated on a slope have great potential to be particularly attractive. For a start, they usually have glorious views, even if they make considerable demands in terms of imagination, design and commitment. On any sloping piece of ground the work involved will entirely depend on the size of the garden, the surface and steepness of the incline as well as your individual ideas. Three options are available.

Retaining walls

A retaining wall or stretch of wooden palisades can divide a slope into two levels. The walls can be built using mortar, but for a diversity of plant and animal life, dry stone walls are better. Not only the coping of a dry stone wall but also the gaps between the courses can be filled with fragrant cushion-forming and herbaceous rockery perennials. Whether hewn or unhewn natural stone, artificial stones or frost-resistant bricks are used for the walls, the same or a matching material should be chosen for the path. Wall recesses provide a particularly enchanting location for a sheltered seating area.

Herbaceous perennials for sunny wall copings

▷ Cat's claws (*Anthyllis montana*)
▷ Dalmatian bellflower (*Campanula portenschlagiana*)
▷ Creeping baby's breath (*Gypsophila repens*)
▷ Moss phlox (*Phlox subulata* hybrids)
▷ Giant flowering soapwort (*Saponaria × lempergii*)
▷ Low sedum varieties

Top: *This gracefully curved dry stone wall divides the garden into two levels. Golden flax* (Linum flavum) *spills over the stony coping.*
Above: *Rockery gardens can take many forms and can be sited in shady and moist sloping areas, as well as hot, dry, flat places interspersed with rocks. Pictured here is a flowerbed with plants that would normally live in stony leys and flourish in dry conditions, such as yellow asphodel* (Asphodeline lutea), *pink sunrose* (Helianthemum 'Rosi'), *and cushion milkweed* (Euphorbia polychroma) *as well as white and blue perennial flax* (Linum perenne).

Terracing

Steep slopes that have a gradient of over 45 degrees are best terraced using several walls to create flat surfaces for flowerbeds at several different levels. Depending on the width of these terraces, steps and a path should be put in to provide easy access. The terraces can be formal in planting and shape or they can be freer in style. With the latter, have the retaining walls made in staggered, gently sweeping arcs to provide room for flowerbeds or an open seating area. Create a wonderful hanging-garden effect by planting trailing plants such as aubrieta and geraniums over the edges, or ease them into the gaps between the stones or bricks.

Rock gardens

Southern slopes, often also the site of the patio, offer the ideal conditions for a rock garden. Different-sized stone blocks can be used to contain the slope and should be laid with their widest, heavy side in the ground. Perhaps also acting as stepping stones. Most rock garden plants require a very well-drained gritty soil that is not too rich in nutrients. Whether the soil contains lime or not will influence the choice of plants. The construction of the rock garden, the choice of stones and the preparation of the soil, which if clayey or compacted may require drainage, have to be carried out with the same care given to choosing the plants.

Sloping fragrant flowerbeds in a formal terraced setting. The attractive sloping design is solidly defined and enhanced by the evergreen clipped hedge and spherical box features, while the individual flowerbeds exude the delicate fragrances of lavender and roses.

Garden and Flowerbed Styles

The style you use in your garden and flowerbeds will create
different atmospheres that will reflect your individuality,
ideas and preferences. Features and plants can be
arranged in the geometrical fashion of a formal garden or
in a more freestyle form (left-hand page). Whether you
choose to create structured order or experiment freely with
colour and shapes (above) or even try and imitate nature,
your garden will always be uniquely yours.

Classical Formal Flowerbeds

Key classic features

Formal gardens are architectural, plant-incorporating structures. Just as a house is divided into rooms, the garden is divided into distinct areas. Formal designs are based on the following criteria: symmetry, geometry, perspective and pattern. Usually a wide pathway acts as the symmetrical axis, providing the connection between house and garden. To this axis are added symmetrical geometric forms such as circles, squares, rectangles or octagons which are filled with flowerbeds, lawns or water features, all connected by paths, leafy walkways, hedges or avenues. These provide for vertical features in the garden and together with other artistic eyecatching elements are used to attract attention. The patterns of the flowerbeds, and the individual beds themselves, reveal the gardener's true skill in ornamentation. Nothing is random in a formal classical garden symbolizing man's control over nature. Over the centuries the principles remained the same, yet flowerbed design has been witness to many interesting developments.

Renaissance flowerbeds

A variation of this theme were the Italian Renaissance gardens. Composed of three parts – the flower garden, the fruit garden and the copse – they were arranged in a structured order and enclosed by walls. The flower gardens were made up of chessboard-style rectangular flowerbeds or highly complex knot beds and specially constructed terraces or hills which provided platforms to enjoy the patterns of the flowerbeds below. During the 16th and early 17th centuries, many new and highly prized plants found their way into European gardens. To show them off and as a sign of their wealth, nobles and princes created flower gardens following the Italian model. Flowering plants were generally presented in square compartments framed with stones, bricks, wood or herbs. They were planted in individual beds of just one species, one colour or according to a set mixed pattern to create the impression of a colourful patterned carpet. Planting was in orderly rows, following the principles of 'massing' and 'mingling', which were observed until the turn of the 19th century.

Although still thought of as formal, knot beds, by contrast, consisted of highly complicated planting schemes. Low hedges were made from fragrant herbs, such as hyssop, thyme, rosemary, cotton lavender, box and winter savoury, and were kept in shape by regular trimming. The spaces in between the so-called 'open' knots were filled with inorganic materials such as sand, gravel or coal dust whereas low-growing flowering plants were used for the 'closed' knots. Ornaments in the shape of shields or initials were also popular.

Baroque flowerbeds

Box (*Buxus sempervirens*), hitherto scorned because of its strong aroma, became very popular as a framing plant for flowerbeds during the 17th century, and from this developed embroidery beds, *parterres de broderie*, which were surrounded with low box hedges. Very like

knot gardens, parterres dispensed with angular patterns and took the form of stylized plants or the heads of birds and dragons. Colour was sometimes used in the spaces in between but this was not created with flowers, as is often the case in today's baroque gardens. As in the Renaissance, flowerbeds were essentially flat but they were less colourful. The next breakthrough was the *parterre d'eau*, the new water garden from France, in which the water was divided into rows of compartments using channels.

Victorian flowerbeds

During the 18th century, formal gardens became less popular and garden makers began to look to nature for inspiration (see page 40 for more information). However, by the mid-19th century they had come back into fashion again. With their geometric layouts, they proved ideal for the small front gardens that were typical of Victorian terraces, while the advent of heated greenhouses fulfilled the huge demand for exotic annuals that could be used to fill the gardens. This gave rise to three types of flowerbed:

▷ Flowerbeds containing summer flowers planted in large numbers according to the 'massing' principle.

▷ Ribbon flowerbeds with planting in stripes and patterns.

▷ Carpet-like flowerbeds with dense combinations of annual leafy plants.

At the start of the 19th century a new passion for roses led to the first formal gardens made exclusively for roses, their exuberance contrasting with their more austere box frames (above). In the Renaissance and baroque periods, roses were used as a boundary hedge or on a trellis as well as in flowerbeds mixed with summer and bulb flowers.

Modern Formal Flowerbeds

Above: *A delightful grassy mound of miscanthus (Miscanthus sinensis 'Malepartus')
surrounded by low palm branch sedge (Carex muskingumensis).*
Below: *This shrub bed has different-sized box spheres under a trellis of woven lime (Tilia)
branches (see also page 53).*

Even William Robinson (1838–1935), who
paved the way for freer designs with his move
away from formal gardens and the unnatural
'wedding cake style' of Victorian summer
bedding, admitted that flowerbeds near to the
house should follow certain structural
principles, in order to sit more comfortably
with the house. He realized that formal designs
radiate calm with their strong sense of
structure and composition. This has since been
proved time and again, especially in small
gardens with their close relationship to the
house. It is no surprise that even today, when
creating an attractive garden to relax in, garden
designers often turn to this traditional style,
although we do usually modify it considerably
to suit modern ideas.

From rejection to a new direction

It is surprising how often contemporary garden
design shows traces of formality, even though
much of it is based on ideas that are rooted in a
rejection of the ornamental style of the 19th
century. However, whereas using large quantities
of plants, planted en masse, had been the main
tool for colourful ornamentation in the 16th and
17th century, modern garden designers focus on
the expressive power and individuality of each
plant. They are inspired by Impressionism and
Symbolism as well as by Chinese and Japanese
gardens. The type of plant and the shapes,
colours and textures of the leaves have become
the most important design consideration.

Modern design

Modern formal flowerbeds tend to use sharp boundaries both internally and at their edges. Here are a few typical examples for using plants in a modern setting:

▷ The solitary feature. Like minimalist architecture, a single plant can have a strikingly effective, atmospheric silhouette. The Swiss Henri Correvon (1853–1922) made a list of 'architectural plants' that could be used to dominate flowerbeds with their striking forms or the shapes of their leaves. It includes ornamental grasses, plants with sword-like leaves such as yucca, New Zealand flax (*Phormium*) and iris, large-leaved plants such as the umbrella plant (*Darmera peltata*) or plants with distinctively straight growths, such as the red hot poker (*Kniphofia*), cotton thistle (*Onopodium acanthium*) and mullein (*Verbascum*).

▷ Place plants with similar foliage in rows or groups to increase and intensify the overall effects of the planting.

▷ You do not need to make flat flowerbeds conform to the basic pattern of traditional formal gardens; try different shapes, for example cube-shaped box beds.

▷ Make use of contrasts. Plants can be contrasted with unusual surfaces, creating a new visual stimulus or even showing the plant in a completely different light. A uniform background is often sufficient to achieve this effect, for example plain walls or walls of one colour. Chessboard flowerbeds are also popular, set against concrete slabs, gravel or coloured glass granules. Particularly arresting reflections can be created by plants in lines in concrete containers set in still water.

This small garden seems to be playing lightheartedly with historical fashions. While its division into identical compartments of flowers is reminiscent of the Renaissance style, the plants used tend towards the Victorian penchant for tall-stemmed roses and carpet-like flowerbeds. The modern and innovative touch is the rejection of patterns and the use of only two colours: blue-violet lavender (Lavandula angustifolia 'Munstead') and snow-white standard roses.

Formal Elements in Informal Designs

Above: *Calm, yet rippling like waves, these formal yew hedges create a harmonious background for the natural-looking flowerbeds.*
Below: *The parade of mop-head acacia (Robinia pseudoacacia 'Umbraculifera') between freely arranged borders is reminiscent of Renaissance gardens.*

Classical guidelines for a formal garden have many interpretations giving almost unlimited scope for freer, more individual designs. Perhaps it is their formal structure combined with their flexibility that is the secret of their enduring popularity. The possibilities for combining formal shapes and elements with more freely designed ones are endless and can produce truly enchanting garden compositions.

Combining formal and informal

Traditional plants and materials, formal flowerbed shapes and borders, lines of sight, symmetry and trimmed plant sculptures can lend a classical formal aura to one part of the garden, perhaps near the house, and this can then open out into a more loosely designed or natural section further away towards the boundaries. For a harmonious transition, choose matching plants and colours for both sides. On the other hand, you could make intentional contrasts to create a more striking effect.

Using formal frames

Formally clipped hedges can serve as green walls providing a uniform backdrop for informal borders, corner flowerbeds or any other ornamental arrangement of plants. The inner area of the garden will also gain a solid, three-dimensional feel if you use hedges to act as screens, dividing the garden into small chambers. This will in turn increase the impact of the plants and flowers in the beds.

Low or short hedges which cut in with wave-like or other free form shapes are an excellent way to make a variety of areas for housing flowerbeds, seating areas or water features. Furthermore, the restful appearance of low clipped hedges or borders is ideal for setting off a lively flowerbed. Box borders provide the finishing touches for summer flowers and vegetables, especially filigreed herbs and irregularly twisting roses. The more mixed and uneven the plants in the flowerbed, the more agreeable a regular unifying strip will seem.

Cherry-picking formal features

Give free rein to your imagination when you use formal elements. Any of them can be used as a striking feature. Combinations which pair potted plants, clipped box spirals or pyramids with climbing plants or small spherical trees can highlight paths, entrances and pavilions. Placed within flowerbeds, box sculptures, such as spheres, cones, cubes or cuboids, give stability to uneven planting and ensure a sense of balance as their strong forms will dominate the scene.

Above: *A yew cone asserts itself as a pillar of calm among the wild, shady planting of plantain lilies* (Hosta) *and blue creeping comfrey* (Symphytum grandiflorum *'Hidcote Blue'*).
Below: *Two imposing spherically shaped ground cherries* (Prunus fruticosa) *guard the entrance to a new part of the garden.*

Formal Elements in Informal Designs   37

Making Formal Flowerbeds

Top left: *This circular flowerbed rejects everything angular, featuring a rounded brick paved area and spherical box edging.*
Top right: *Set against bulbous yew hedges, the perfect squares of the linear box frame neatly set off and contain plantain lilies (Hosta) with their attractive leaf colours and shapes.*
Below left: *A crossroads of paths lined with rue (Ruta graveolens 'Jackman's Blue').*
Below right: *This flowerbed is delineated by and contained within the raised edging of natural stone instead of plants.*

Deciding on a shape

The simplest forms of formal flowerbed, which are found time and again in modern gardens, are rectangles, squares, rhombuses, circles and ovals. These can lie either side of a symmetrical axis, or have the axis cut through them, or form a quartet of flowerbeds if another axis is added at right angles.

It may sound complicated, but it is nothing more than the basic idea of four flowerbeds and a crossroads. The centre of the crossroads can also include an additional circular flowerbed, a round pond area, an octagonal or circular arbour, a rhombus or even something without plants such as a bird bath, a plant container or a sundial.

Roy Strong, a specialist in Renaissance and formal gardens, points out that at any given time the patterns used in decorative art are very similar, 'whether textiles, print, wallpaper, ceramics, furniture or the garden'. So he designs flowerbeds based on art deco patterns or uses a painting by a famous artist as an outline. He recommends the op art of the 1960s as another treasure trove for designs for modern formal gardens.

Above left: A blossoming border of iris and tulips. The narrow, pointed iris leaves provide structure throughout the winter and conceal the dwindling foliage of the tulips after flowering.

Above right: The tulips ('Red Appledoorn') flank the path with natural grace. Various summer flowers then take on the role of providing a succession of colour in the border.

Below left: Coloured foliage can add a splash of colour to the border from spring until autumn, as proved by these coral bells (Heuchera 'Stormy Seas') with their frilly red foliage.

Below right: Instead of a raised border, bricks are set in several rows at ground level to define the edge of the flowerbed.

Edging

What would formal flowerbeds be without the finishing touches? Suited to both sun and shade, box (*Buxus sempervirens* 'Suffruticosa') can be trimmed into angular or semi-circular shapes or into rows of spheres or cubes. With its air of order and durability, even in winter and under snow, clipped box will ensure your compositions have a sense of tranquility all year round.

Evergreen subshrubs are also suitable for edging in sunny sites and are easy to keep trimmed into shape. Suitable plants include wall germander (*Teucrium chamaedrys*), common rue (*Ruta*

graveolens*) and lavender (*Lavandula angustifolia*). Alternatively, use bushy, low-growing herbaceous perennials, such as wormwood (*Artemisia schmidtiana* 'Nana') or catmint (*Nepeta* x *faassenii*) to create a row of plants with more variety. Iris (*Iris barbata* hybrids) and bergenias (*Bergenia* hybrids) with their evergreen foliage can also create a more permanent structure with a freer form.

If you are looking for a flowering border, annuals such as the scented sweet alyssum (*Lobularia maritima*) or marigolds can be used to provide delightful colours throughout the summer.

Informal Flowerbeds

Delicate colours and tones combined with bolder flower colours and shapes turn this flowerbed into a truly splendid floral painting.

It was the landscape painting style of the 17th century that was responsible for introducing the concept of the natural into the garden. Arcadian landscapes painted by the likes of Claude Lorrain and Nicolas Poussin were the models for the English landscape garden. While perhaps the greatest source of inspiration for the style was Alexander Pope (1688–1744), who favoured gardens that were free from artificiality. Formality lived on in the flowerbeds near to the house, but an idealized version of nature, as found in a panoramic painting, became more and more popular for areas of the garden beyond this. The effects were achieved by altering the landscape and making water features, bridges and classically inspired follies and pavilions as well as trying to create a wild ambience with the judicious use of trees and shrubs. These were usually planted sparsely to create open parkland and their inclusion was integral to the creation of picturesque scenes, intended to stir the emotions. At the end of the 18th century a debate began over the meaning of the word 'picturesque' and it was decided that it should reflect the reality of nature more closely, with less structured vegetation and a wilder landscape.

Naturalism and the cottage garden

Towards the end of the 19th century, there was growing concern about the threat to nature caused by industrialization. The Arts and Crafts movement led by John Ruskin (1819–1900) and William Morris (1834–1896) heralded a return to traditional crafts and to the country garden with vegetables, fruits and flowers. Although mainly still planted in formally styled grounds and flowerbeds, indigenous and exotic plants, mostly hardy herbaceous perennials and bulbs, would be used to create natural, 'picturesque' designs in delicate, subtle colours.

Influenced by the Naturalism movement, William Robinson (1838–1935) further developed the concept of a free, natural and yet aesthetic arrangement of plants in his book *The English Flower Garden* (1883), which is still relevant today:

▷ Trimmed shrubs are shunned as they appear too unnatural.

▷ Hardy herbaceous perennials and bulbs become the focus of attention because the flowerbeds are planted so as to be informal for as long as possible.

▷ Complementary herbaceous perennials should be grouped together as naturally as possible.

▷ Bedding plants are especially recommended.

▷ Bulb flowers are advocated for naturalizing in grass.

▷ The use of natural-looking clematis and other climbers to swathe around trees is encouraged. Gertrude Jekyll (1843–1932) is famous for her adoption and development of these ideas.

Freestyle flowerbeds

In informal and cottage-style gardens, order and structure are pushed aside in favour of allowing the plants to provide the atmosphere all year round with their different forms, the shapes of their leaves and flowers, their textures and colours. The approach aims to make the most of individual plants by combining and perhaps juxtaposing them to reveal their distinctive and often contrasting character. This is a very good way to create seasonal compositions. Freestyle effects can be achieved with beds consisting purely of annuals, shrubs or herbaceous perennials or with combined mixed plantings.

Top: *A herbaceous perennial bed in autumn set against brilliant silvery tufts of pampas grass (Cortaderia selloana).* Above: *A shrub bed benefiting from the various colours of Indian bean tree (Catalpa bignonioides), red smoke tree (Cotinus coggygria 'Royal Purple'), bluebeard (Caryopteris x clandonensis) and hydrangea (Hydrangea 'Annabelle').*

*This mixed planting
creates interesting effects
using pink. Hollyhocks
(Alcea) and giant
bellflowers (Campanula
lactiflora 'Loddon Anna')
create the background for
the low-growing shrub rose
'Bonica' and rose campion
(Lychnis coronaria).*

Gertrude Jekyll, the originator of subtle but colourful flowerbeds, often still had formal layouts but she stopped planting box borders and instead used swirls of plants for a looser edge to the flowerbed. Completely free design tends towards natural flowerbed shapes. Their contours are seldom straight but rather gently flowing and often curved. Their irregular appearance is accentuated by adding plants that are allowed to overhang the edges of the bed.

In such designs the principle of 'artistic similarity' – the 'massing' of plants – is also dropped in favour of a diversity of plants. The designer creates highlights by mixing combinations of plants in small and large groups. There is a rejection of the idea of having a carpet of one colour and height, and designers revel in the use of different heights to create a variety of silhouettes. These fit naturally into the garden, although the flowerbeds remain independent elements within the design.

Freedom and form

If a natural-looking, completely unstructured garden is not what is wanted, informal flowerbeds also benefit from a framework or structure to guide the eye and reveal the design. There are various ways of doing this:

▷ subordinating, grouping and repeating colours and shapes

▷ setting the flowerbeds against the calming green of a grassy surface

▷ returning to formal plot patterns as frames and borders.

A perfect balance between the opposing aspects of freedom and form is exemplified in 20th-century Dutch garden design using perennials. In the 1920s, the art movement known as 'De Stijl' emerged in the Netherlands, and this shifted the emphasis in garden design towards an orderly framework and stability through simplicity, linearity and the use of primary colours in flowerbed compositions.

And then, towards the end of the 20th century, Piet Oudolf paved the way for a new style that would meet with enthusiasm far beyond the borders of Europe, by taking a quite different approach. He extended the creative possibilities in plants by using grasses and wild herbaceous perennials. His landscapes proclaim the beauty and diversity of nature showing a penchant for subtle colours, natural forms and expressive leaf shapes. The freer and more complex his arrangements with shapes, textures and colour become, however, the more he embeds his them in structural, formal surroundings.

A masterful late-summer display by Piet Oudolf, featuring some of his favourite plants in a progressive grouping, from left to right: alpine eryngo (Eryngium alpinum), sneezeweed (Helenium hybrid), black false hellebore (Veratrum nigrum), bistort (Persicaria amplexicaulis) and purple coneflower (Echinacea purpurea 'Rubinstern').

Close to Nature – Wild Flowers

Considered to be the father of the natural use of plants, William Robinson made the following comment about planting narcissi (his declared favourites): 'To scatter Narcissi equally over the grass everywhere is to destroy all chance of repose, of relief, and of seeing them in the ways in which they often arrange themselves.' He recommends following the shapes of small clouds in the sky as a guide to grouping them. A sea of glory of the snow (Chionodoxa) provides the perfect foil for the daffodils.

Gardens that are close to nature are, from a planting point of view, an extension of informal design but have a different emphasis. In contrast to deliberate and structured gardens which are often rich in colour and can be stunning but do stand out from their surroundings, the natural arrangement of plants in their appropriate environment is of paramount importance in wild gardens. But even these plantings are the artistic creations of human beings; they are not the same as truly natural areas. To describe this method of imitating nature, the well-known German nurseryman Karl Foerster coined the term 'wilderness garden art'.

Siting natural flowerbeds

Natural flowerbeds require a suitable milieu. They are best in large gardens, or gardens with a wild or natural setting, and for any areas that are far away from buildings. They can form an artistic contrast in part of a large but otherwise more structured garden. There are various reasons for choosing natural flowerbeds:

▷ To help achieve an enchanting garden that contains all the wild sensual qualities of the natural plant world and expresses something of its magnificent diversity.

▷ To increase the range of animals, birds and plants that you see in your own garden so that you witness the interaction between them, and thus enhance your enjoyment of the garden.

▷ To reduce the amount of time you spend working in your garden through less labour-

Right-hand page:
*This magically varied corner has an informal layout with wild herbaceous perennials planted in the damp, partially shaded area: colour-co-ordinated meadow rue (*Thalictrum aquilegifolium)*, bistort (*Persicaria)* and wood cranesbill (*Geranium sylvaticum) create a harmonious scene.*
Below: *A natural experience Japanese-style. Japanese maple (*Acer japonicum) *and royal fern (*Osmunda regalis) *in glowing autumn colours.*

intensive plantings that will develop their own interesting dynamic without much assistance.

▷ To enhance difficult sites in the garden, such as shady areas, places where the roots of trees provide too much competition, and excessively wet or dry areas, where demanding decorative plantings would be unable to flourish or could only be sustained with a very high level of commitment.

Making 'natural' planting schemes

An important distinguishing feature between formal and wild flowerbeds is that natural plantings do not represent a separate design feature but are seamlessly integrated into the surrounding garden, with the aim of providing a mirror of nature or dramatically heightened portrayal of it. Plantings at the edge of a pond or on a dry stone area or plantings in front of a shrub border away from the sun achieve their beauty by looking as if they have developed naturally. For example, try spring-flowering plants below and in front of shrubs, arranging them very loosely so they look as if they had grown there by themselves or throw narcissus bulbs over the lawn and plant them where they land. In these cases, there is no flowerbed, but the area is enriched by the planting. When choosing plants, select wild plants typical of your local area – or use improved varieties instead of wild species – as they are sure to flourish in the conditions in your garden and are more likely to fit in with existing indigenous varieties. Large-leaved herbaceous perennials are found in damp areas while juniper, heather and birch immediately bring moorland to mind.

Plant selection boils down to a question of long-living herbaceous perennials and shrubs with a wild character. These impress not so much with their flowers but rather with their very robustness, their leaves and their shape. To show wild plantings in the best possible light, mix indigenous plants with plants from abroad that need a similar environment. Plant tall herbaceous perennials as solitary features or far apart and fill the gaps in between with medium-height and low herbaceous perennials in mixed groups. In this way you will create stunning garden scenes full of natural beauty.

How to Use Flowerbeds

Just like architectural elements, flowerbeds contribute to the
overall effect of the garden. They can emphasize the
horizontal, exude romantic perfume and, when given a
formal outline, become a prominent focal point, like this
fragrant bed (above) filled with chamomile (Chamaemelum
nobile). Or they can structure the garden vertically, making
striking backdrops or dividing up an area with loose
combinations of shrubs and herbaceous perennials (left-hand
page). But flowerbeds are always more than just a way of
showing off plants. They are integral to the garden and give it
seasonal charm, structure and atmosphere.

As Frames

Whether they are formal or freestyle in an overall formal or freestyle garden, flowerbeds can assume various functional roles. In some ways they can be regarded as decorative building blocks.

Their role in the garden

Whether in the sun or the partial shade, flowerbeds can contain plants that scatter the garden with perfume and colour. It is also good to include decoratively leaved plants, bedding plants, ferns and moss to alongside them. Flowerbeds are so versatile that it is no surprise that they are so much appreciated during our leisure hours and are generally sited near our favourite places, so we can savour all of their seductive magic as often as possible. In garden designs, flowerbeds are often found near patios, seating areas, arbours, pavilions, ponds or paths, lining them as a frame or edging.

The shape decides the style

Flowerbeds can be used to enclose entire garden areas. Those with a regular shape can create a formal, strip-like frame, while those with irregular, sweeping contours produce a rather more loose liberated effect. Using flowerbeds as frames for a seating area and beside patios will determine the whole style of the area, either making it free and natural in feel or more structured and contained.

Most seating areas work best when they have some sort of screening behind and to the side, while the view at the front is open. Here, Japanese dogwood (Cornus kousa) and rhododendrons provide a delightful backdrop. The floral and leafy splendour of rodgersia (Rodgersia podophylla) on one side and bush roses, bellflowers and box spheres on the other adds the finishing touches to this secluded, freely styled idyllic spot.

The shape of the flowerbed can also create a different sense of perspective. Borders of equal width, for example, running either side of a long narrow area can make it appear even narrower. If, however, their edges are softened and allowed to encroach into the area they frame, they will make it appear substantially wider.

Deciding on the plants

The choice of plants must always be appropriate to the location. While framing borders are normally planted in gradually increasing height, it is advisable to plant flowerbeds next to seating areas and patios with lower plants to allow a few lines of sight into the garden.

Flowerbeds that are intended as frames around patios or entire sections of the garden should be attractive all year round. Continuously blooming flowerbeds require the highest level of gardening skills, however, you can produce wonderful results by using the following simple trick: give structure to the bed by planting evergreens such as box, lavender, iris or small conifers, surrounding them with perfumed roses, perennials that have different flowering times and annuals.

In modern courtyards and atrium gardens, minimalist framing flowerbeds can be most striking. For example, alternating gravel areas with plants that have a strong shape such as grasses, cushions of moss or topiary box.

This border between patio and garden edge is somewhat experimental yet has an overall formality. The evergreen ivy and box spheres guarantee year-round beauty in the geometrical patio flowerbeds. Together with the lawn, they create a calming and cooling effect, toning down the exuberance of the mixed borders.

As Decorative Screens

Below: *Plants in containers and on walls can provide attractive screening, as in this sumptuous floral sea of pelargoniums and culver's root (*Veronicastrum virginicum *var.* incarnatum)
Bottom: *Magnificent and impossible to see through – evergreen rhododendrons.*

Screening is usually a necessity within the garden if you want to create intimate seclusion for a seating area, arbour or any quiet area; it is also vital that adequate screening is provided at the garden boundaries to prevent onlookers. There is good screening potential in:
▷ several rows of tall herbaceous plants
▷ free-growing flowering hedges
▷ clipped hedges
▷ woven hedges
▷ trellises, railings, pergolas and fences covered in climbing plants.

A question of space

Whether they stretch continuously along the edges of the garden or are curved around a seating area, beds of tall perennials and unclipped hedges require a lot more space than closely maintained hedges or climbing plants on trellises. Flowerbeds around a seating area should be at least 1.2m (4ft) wide so that the roses, tall herbaceous perennials and annuals all have the space they need to grow and display themselves to their full potential.

For unclipped hedges, a trench of 60cm (24in) wide is sufficient for planting the root balls. However, these hedges need to be allowed to become quite bushy and they only really show their true beauty when a flower border is planted in front of them, so a better bed width would be at least 2.5m (8ft).

Wild hedges are planted several rows deep with gaps in between. Usually individual holes are made for each shrub as they are fairly robust and can cope with difficult conditions. Clipped hedges, woven hedges and climbing plants on trellises can cope with a bed width of only 60cm (24in) as long as they do not have to compete with any planting in front of them. Do not be tempted to reduce the widths of the beds otherwise the plants will not thrive and the area will never look its best.

For a topiary hedge, dig out a 60cm (24in) wide trench at least 30cm (12in) deep. This will ensure that the hedge, which will be densely planted, has good growing conditions and a plentiful supply of nutrients.

If any flowerbeds are placed in front of hedges that are to be clipped, remember to allow space for an access path so the hedge can be cut when necessary and to allow the plants at the back to be tended.

Tips for planning hedges and beds

Mark out the course for clipped hedges with a length of string. If curving flowerbeds are to be laid in front of the hedge, mark their outlines with a garden hose so that you can get them exactly as you want them before cutting them out of the turf. Remove weed roots before planting hedges and flowers.

Fabulous forms for limited space

A decorative and space-saving screen can be provided by woven hedges fixed to a framework. Posts are anchored 2.5m (8ft) apart and at least 60cm (24in) deep in the ground, linked together with horizontal slats at three or more different levels. The shrubs are planted against the vertical posts and their side branches are interwoven into the horizontal slats to which they are fixed.

Suitable trees for a woven hedge

Three- to four-year-old trees in each case with straight, strong trunks:

▷ European hornbeam (*Carpinus betulus*)

▷ Common beech (*Fagus sylvatica*)

▷ Lime trees (*Tilia* species)

▷ London plane (*Platanus* x *hispanica*)

▷ Common holly (*Ilex aquifolium*)

Woven hedges like the one above, using the slender trunks of the lime trees for posts, can be planted directly underneath with shade-tolerant shrubs. The layered planting features different highlights all year round. Thick-rooted cranesbill (Geranium macrorrhizum, front) flowers from early summer to midsummer to be followed by the hydrangea behind, whose yellow autumn foliage gloriously complements the brilliant red of the cotoneaster (Cotoneaster horizontalis).

To Divide Areas

The informal flowerbeds that separate this patio from the garden are very eyecatching and, along with the double feature of the mop-head acacia (Robinia pseudoacacia 'Umbraculifera'), soften the hard landscaping.

Flowerbeds do not have to adjoin house or perimeter walls, hedges or fences. They can also be used as independent features and are very effective when they divide up the garden two- or three-dimensionally with their outlines and height, thus providing separate areas of interest, hidden from the direct view of the house. With uniform low planting, they can be placed in a straight line, as a decorative band or as a flat carpet so as to create a strong horizontal structure. Alternatively, use taller planting, for example ornamental shrubs, roses and tall herbaceous perennials, or with green trellis walls, to make the scene much more three-dimensional. By adding large flowerbeds on one or both sides of a lawn, you can create individual garden areas, which can then be used or planted in quite different ways. Smaller flowerbeds that cross the garden widthways can break up the centralized focus, helping to reinforce the three-dimensional effect using foreground, middle and background.

Just one, or a mixture of styles?

In classical formal gardens, tall or low clipped hedges as well as structured flowerbeds with box borders can be carved symmetrically on both sides of an area. In modern gardens, these dividers can also be used on one or both sides as well as appearing at intervals. With uniform planting (for example, bedding plants and shaped evergreens) and strong geometrical forms (for example, rectangles, squares, triangles) their formal appearance will provide structure in any colourful or free planting.

In freestyle designs, on the other hand, the flowerbeds can be made almost any shape, with irregular outlines and sweeping, tall silhouettes created by the plants. Placing these beside a lush green lawn will provide a sense of tranquillity and ensure that one feature enhances the other.

A very original effect can be achieved through imaginative combinations of elements from both styles. The contours of the flowerbeds can be naturally curved, but with a strongly regimented planting, such as in the photograph on the right.

Design tips

▷ Dividers made from evergreen shrubs have the capacity to give shape all year round.

▷ A garden becomes full of interesting diversity when the surfaces of the planted flowerbeds (full surfaces) and the lawn (empty surfaces) are not the same size.

▷ Small gardens are made to feel larger by disguising their boundaries, which can be done by planting shrubs and tall plants along them.

▷ Even freely arranged flowerbeds have a strong structuring effect when they divide the garden on two sides and create a line of sight using pairs of vertical elements, for example neatly shaped shrubs, green trimmed sculptures, tall-stemmed plants, covered obelisks, planted bowls on top of columns or rose arches.

Above: *Here, clipped hedges are not dividing up the garden but rather dividing up the bed.*
Below: *This 'bubbly' bed swings out into the lawn. Small works of evergreen art made from box spheres and yew sculptures alternate in an original mix of styles.*

As Striking Features

Above: *A formal carpet-like flowerbed with a colourful planting of stonecrop (*Sedum pluricaule*), topiary box cones and white* Gaura lindheimeri.
Below: *An ivy mat overrun with ornamental onion is the perfect surface for presenting the jewel-like bonsai.*
Right-hand page: *An informal flowerbed under corkscrew willow with creeeping euonymus (*Euonymus fortunei *'Variegatus') and stinking hellebore (*Helleborus foetidus*).*

Any plant can become a captivating garden feature. To achieve this, the plant should be strikingly arranged in a contrasting frame where its unusual or surprising appearance will engage the attention of all.

Contrasting layouts

Flowerbeds can draw attention to themselves because of their unique setting within contrasting surroundings. An island bed amid the flat green of a lawn will instantly become an exciting feature:

▷ when it lies centrally (principle: fixed central point)
▷ when its outline has a strong geometrical shape
▷ when a vertical element – plant or decoration – attracts the eye or the flowerbed itself is laid out at different heights (principle: horizontal against vertical)
▷ when the flowerbed clearly contrasts with the lawn due to its colour (principle: colour against colour).

To be striking a feature must be solitary. If a flowerbed is repeated and grouped with several others, it will lose its effect and will then only function as part of an ensemble with the other flowerbeds.

When designing a flowerbed as a feature, you do not have to include all the above criteria. The interplay between the similar and contrasting properties of the plants and the surroundings is a never-ending source of new and enchanting combinations.

An island bed is already eyecatching because of its position but it can be made even more attention-grabbing through the use of arches, paths, tall-stemmed flowers, topiary and other features. The main feature of this circular flowerbed is a graceful tamarisk (Tamarix) with a dark red carpet of coral bells (Heuchera 'Stormy Seas') and filigreed ornamental grasses at its base.

For Fragrance

Creating an ambience

The most important task of fragrance in the garden is to intensify our overall enjoyment of the garden experience, creating varying ambiences and producing different emotions and atmospheres.

Perfumed flowers and aromatic leaves make a vital contribution to any flowerbed. As well as improving our feeling of well-being, they will also entice a rich variety of insects into the garden. Annuals, herbaceous perennials, bulb flowers, herbs, roses, shrubs, trees, potted plants and climbers (see table on page 128) all include plants that have entrancing perfumes.

Scent all year round

By making fragrant plantings you can arrange little sensual highlights throughout the garden, their positions varying according to the time of the year. Ideally such plantings should be in places where you spend a lot of time or frequently pass by, such as beside a patio or other areas near to the house, then they can impart their sweet fragrances for all to enjoy.

There is a particularly extensive range of aromatic and fragrant plants available for sunny places. Alternatively, you can choose those that only begin to exude their perfumes in the evening, creating truly romantic summer nights. Seating areas in the garden are often positioned in the partial shade or full shade to provide refreshing coolness during a hot summer and there is a wonderful assortment of fragrant

shrubs and climbing plants that thrive in these conditions. By placing perfumed plants beside seating areas or at eye level, you will be able to really enjoy the flower displays and at the same time savour all the delightful fragrances. Sunken gardens, terraces or recesses in walls are ideal for creating raised flowerbeds that enable plants to be experienced from a completely new perspective.

Perfumed climbing shrubs such as rambling or climbing roses, wisteria, honeysuckle or vines look most attractive on pergolas, arbours or leafy walkways and release sweet showers of fragrances from above which will tantalize the senses. Their often rather bare bases can be swathed in a fragrant accompaniment of lavender, lilies or carnations to create beautiful sweet-smelling oases.

Fragrances can also rise upwards from the ground below, for example from flowerbeds flanking a path. For a particularly heady effect, plant a path with aromatic herbs that you can walk on. By treading on chamomile (*Chamaemelum nobile* 'Treneague'), wild thyme (*Thymus serpyllum*), *Leptinella potentillina* or Corsican mint (*Mentha requienii*), you will release clouds of spicy, intoxicating aromas into the air as you walk by.

Left-hand page top: *Roses and lavender line the edge of the flowerbed, creating a classical bouquet of delightful fragrances.*
Left-hand page bottom: *Richly scented regal lilies* (Lilium regale) *accompanied by lamb's ears* (Stachys byzantina) *and delphiniums in a walled planting.*
Above: *This wisteria is woven into a leafy walkway and in late spring to early summer exudes the heavenly scent of vanilla.*

In Kitchen Gardens

Vegetables, herbs and fruits are becoming increasingly popular, and they can be planted alone, together or even combined with ornamental plants in decorative flowerbeds. In very small gardens – the norm in modern homes – there is often not enough room for separate decorative and productive beds. So why not combine the two and make a gourmet garden!

Removing boundaries

Dreary vegetable plots are a thing of the past. Eschewing the conventional divide between ornamental and edible plants should inspire the gardener to transform the colours and shapes of the leaves and the textures of vegetables and herbs into truly splendid designs, especially as the number of vegetables with brightly coloured foliage is increasing. Some delightful plantings can be achieved when they are planted alone or with flowers for an even more elegant effect.

▷ Create vertical features by planting runner beans, peas, climbing strawberries on obelisks, tall-stemmed berries, spindle trees or column-shaped Ballerina apple cultivars to prevent flowerbeds from turning into boring carpets.

▷ Use chives, lavender, curry plant (*Helichrysum italicum*) or nasturtiums for a variation on the conventional flowerbed.

▷ Use tall edible plants with an imposing presence as solitary plants, for example artichokes, cardoon (*Cynara cardunculus*), angelica (*Angelica archangelica*) or purple fennel (*Foeniculum vulgare* 'Atropurpureum').

▷ Plant brightly coloured vegetables and herbs to enhance purely decorative beds. Vegetables with longer growing periods are particularly suitable, for example red curly kale 'Redbor', elegant palm cabbage 'Nero di Toscana' or common chard 'Bright Lights' with its rainbow-coloured veins.

Below left: *In the middle of brightly coloured summer flowers, including red zinnia ('Profusion Cherry'), the large show-stopping chard 'Bright Lights' with its darkly glowing, rough leaves demonstrates its magnificent charms.*

Below: *The fragrance from the lavender lingers over this lovely planting featuring a tall-stemmed gooseberry plant. American pokeweed (Phytolacca americana), whose berries were used for colour and decoration, and variegated horseradish (Armoracia rusticana 'Variegata') flank the pathway that leads to the lavender bed.*

The golden hop (Humulus lupulus 'Aureus') will soon transform this arbour into an airy golden-green refuge, with elegant carpet-like flowerbeds at its feet. Red leaf lettuces with ruffled edges and blue-green cabbages with large smooth leaves create a peaceful, even pattern.

DESIGNING FLOWERBEDS

Using Silhouettes and Vertical Features

When planning and planting flowerbeds, think of the heights, the shapes and the silhouettes of the plants as the primary design elements. These will provide the layout and structure, and are generally more enduring than the colours of the flowers. Plants can be used as solitary accents or in groups to create carpet-like blocks or fragrant paths (above). They can even be cleverly arranged to create a raised platform using vertical and round shapes (left-hand page). Their design potential is immense.

Plant Appearance and Design Role

Designing with plants might be likened to working with personalities. The properties of each gives rise to its individual beauty, influenced in turn by its surroundings.

Plant characteristics

The properties of a plant that define a design are its height, form and contours, the colour, shape and size of the flowers and leaves, the length of time it retains its attributes and its surface composition (texture). Because all plants are different in at least one of these aspects, the design possibilities are infinite. Wonderful effects can be created by placing together plants that complement each other in some of these properties but form exciting contrasts in others.

Some design principles

▷ Timing: Colour combinations will only succeed when the plants have the same flowering times. Shrubs, with their enduring shapes, are counted as framework plants. With herbaceous perennials, however, not only the flowering time but also the colour and form of the leaves, their maximum height and spread and the length of their appeal should be considered so that the flowerbed remains attractive even after their blossoms have faded.

▷ Contrast: Combining contrasting properties makes plants appear striking. Ensure that the contrasting pair is not evenly balanced. A column shape, for example, looks better when combined with not one but two spherical silhouettes.

Sunny yellow dominates this flowerbed during early summer. From left to right: yellow corydalis (Corydalis lutea), golden majoram (Origanum vulgare 'Aureum'), lady's mantle (Alchemilla mollis) and at the back the long-stemmed golden flowered columbine (Aquilegia chrysantha). Effects with colour and shape are provided by the white delphinium 'candles' (Delphinium Belladonna Group 'Moerheimii'). Delphiniums are counted among the most popular tall herbaceous perennials, but here the huge privet spheres challenge their pre-eminence and give a structural framework to this gradually ascending flowerbed.

The strong contrasts of leaf and growth forms in this sunny flowerbed are muted by the even more dominant form of the amphora. Distinctive plantings include yellow Sisyrinchium striatum, box spheres, reddish-brown leatherleaf sedge (Carex buchananii), heavenly bamboo (Nandina domestica), black mondo grass (Ophiopogon planiscapus 'Nigrescens'), oriental poppy (Papaver orientale 'Karine') and silver lamb's ears (Stachys byzantina).

▷ Rhythm and repetition: The regular or irregular repetition of groups of shapes and colours within large flowerbeds and borders, as well as within the whole of the garden, will ensure either a striking static feel or a dynamic balanced one.

▷ Reduction: Especially in small gardens, more harmonious effects are achieved by limiting the number of colours and shapes that are used.

Leader, accompaniment or filler?

Flowerbed design is based on the apperance of the plants and makes use of a visual hierarchy. Plants are not ranked according to rigid categories but rather by their function in the flowerbed and their relationship with neighbouring plants.

▷ Leading plants assume the main role in the flowerbed. Tall, striking flowering herbaceous perennials, grasses or ferns occupy this position and are usually distributed individually or in groups throughout the flowerbed, at regular intervals, according to their size and form.

▷ Accompanying plants of medium to low height are placed around the leading perennials and can perform various tasks. They support the leading perennials by having the same flowering times or they might fill the periods before and after with flowers or decorative foliage. In order to achieve this effect, they are always used in larger numbers than the leading perennials.

▷ Filling plants with attractive flowers such as annuals and bulbs are often used to add colourful touches between the groups in the foreground or background. On the other hand, filling plants with decorative forms and foliage, for example grasses and ferns, help to tone down the planting. Bedding plants in the foreground will also achieve the same effect.

This magnificent border of herbaceous perennials gains its striking power through an even, rhythmic repetition of tall groups of purple loosestrife with its sensational violet-red spikes. The flowerbed is resplendent in mid- to late summer, and shows that plants do not have to be arranged by height alone. Large borders can successfully accommodate tall herbaceous perennials even when they are placed in the foreground as an extra element of interest. Most of the herbaceous perennials in this border have a wild character. From left to right: purple loosestrife (Lythrum salicaria), queen of the prairies (Filipendula rubra), long-leaved speedwell (Veronica longifolia), purple loosestrife, golden rod (Solidago hybrid), culver's root (Veronicastrum virginicum 'Alba') and purple loosestrife. The background is extensively planted with Joe Pye weed (Eupatorium purpureum).

70

Above: *Planted only with herbaceous perennials that have a rounded habit, this border is filled with wave-like surges of flowers in a curving, rhythmic, ascending pattern.*

Below: *This rising border is brought alive with a contrast of round and vertical plant shapes. The warm gold and green tones contrast strikingly with the cool silver sprinkles of artemisia.*

Plant Shape and Height

The status and ranking of a plant is decided according to its shape and height. In turn these properties are used to shape the character of the flowerbeds.

The impact of form

The intensity of a plant's form is determined by its silhouette. The more dense the outline, the more powerful its effect in combination. Dense shapes such as spheres, cones or columns, which always have a heavy and dominating effect, are ideal for setting off plants with a more open habit, for example with layered branches. Filigreed grasses or finely branched shrubs introduce an element of further lightness and help to break up the structure. Form is particularly interesting from a design point of view, both alone or in combination:

▷ Thin vertical shapes, such as columnar conifers, large pillar-like herbaceous perennials and tall fountain-like grasses, are dominating features that draw the eye upwards.

▷ Round and domed shapes, such as box spheres or herbaceous perennials with bun-like contours, draw attention to themselves and have a particularly tranquil effect when placed in a lively planting.

▷ Horizontal shapes, such as wide-crowned shrubs, herbaceous perennials like ice plant (*Sedum*) or yarrow (*Achillea*), as well as a variety of bedding plants, do not hold the gaze but rather draw it on towards other features in the garden. To prevent the eye from moving to an

empty space, contrasting plants could be added behind or you might make further horizontal plantings elsewhere in the garden.

▷ Shapes with diagonally rising forms emit liveliness. They give off an aura that goes beyond their own outlines and look most beautiful when they are allowed plenty of space.

Designing with plant forms

Experiment with the layout of every flowerbed using the height and shapes of the plants. Remember that plants which tend to be rather subdued in stature and height will appear more striking in large groups.

▷ Gradually increasing height. Graduating plantings to rise on one side is a great way to display many border plants and ensure they receive sufficient light.

▷ A pyramid or conical formation is excellent for flowerbeds that are to be viewed from all sides. The planting should rise to a central high point.

▷ Wave-shaped plantings work well with the dome-shaped silhouettes of some herbaceous perennials and shrubs. These should be planted in a graduated formation so the height varies only slightly from one plant to the next.

▷ Changing from round to vertical shapes creates particularly vibrant flowerbeds.

▷ Even when they contain patterns of colours or textures, carpet-like flowerbeds appear austere and static due to their uniform height.

The pyramid-style arrangement of a flowerbed can also be produced by mounding soil in the centre. Here, the candle-like flowers of purple loosestrife (Lythrum salicaria) rise up over a fragrant carpet of lavender ('Munstead') with the round flower heads of globe thistle (Echinops ritro) linking the two.

Using Size, Shape and Texture

Captivating designs can also be created by focusing on the leaves and flowers of plants using their shapes, sizes and textures to produce strong contrasts or echoing forms. The planting on around the edge of this seating area (above) exploits the repeated contrast between the size and shape of the leaves of the hydrangea and the privet, whose textures can be described respectively as coarse and fine; they both harmonize with the smooth surface of the table. While the irregular and natural contrast between the medium-textured slim spikes of the bistort (Persicaria amplexicaulis) and the filigreed flowers of the very finely textured white mugwort (Artemisia 'Rosenschleier') (left-hand page) achieves an altogether different effect.

Making the Most of Flowers and Leaves

Flowerbeds designed on the basis of the size and shape of flowers or leaves are most effective when colour assumes a secondary role, in other words in flowerless green or monochrome (single-coloured) plantings.

Using flower shape and size

Even when using a small number of different flowers, you will still find that significant basic structures repeatedly recur, all creating their own unique effect.

▷ Flat plate-like umbels that mainly stay at one height appear horizontal, for example yarrow (*Achillea*), orpine (*Sedum telephium*) ice plant (*S. spectabile*) and Maltese cross (*Lychnis chalcedonica*), as well as large cup flowers with a dense growth, such as coneflower (*Rudbeckia fulgida* var. *sullivantii* 'Goldsturm').

▷ Vertical accents are plentiful and come in all sizes and flowering times: in early summer – delphiniums (*Delphinium*) and lupins (*Lupinus*); in high summer – desert candle (*Eremurus*), mullein (*Verbascum*) or speedwell (*Veronica longifolia*); and in autumn – monkshood (*Aconitum carmichaelii*). The tall, poker-straight blooms of these plants are striking, and make them the indisputable masters of the flowerbed when they are in bloom. In contrast, the shorter, candle-shaped inflorescenses of *Salvia nemorosa* or *Persicaria affinis* are typical of accompanying plants that can be put in an overall flat planting to enhance it with their gentle vertical textures.

▷ Round flowers with their clearly contoured spherical forms, such as ornamental onion (*Allium*) or globe thistle (*Echinops*), can playfully combine with other shapes but also become an attractive feature in their own right.

▷ Pendent flowers, such as bleeding heart (*Dicentra spectabilis*), some day lilies (*Hemerocallis*), montbretia (*Crocosmia*) and many grasses, can only begin to develop their charming sweeping effect when they have enough space.

Below left: In an extravagant contrast of shapes, bear's breeches (Acanthus spinosus) and giant onion (Allium giganteum) enhance the effect of each other's flowers.
Below right: With similar colourings, both the large and small details of the yarrow (Achillea 'Fanal') and sneezeweed (Helenium 'Moerheim Beauty') flowers stand out particularly well.

Designing with flowers and leaves

The same general design rules apply to both flowers and leaves.

▷ Balancing larger features: if you combine large flowers or leaves with smaller ones, the visual weight of the larger shapes should be balanced by using a greater number of smaller shapes.

▷ Contrast of form: arrangements of flowers and leaves can make use of contrast of form. In classical leaf contrasts, referred to by the famous German nurseryman Karl Foerster as 'harps and kettledrums', rounded leaves (*Bergenia* for example, which has large shiny rounded leaves) are set against linear leaves (irises or day lilies, for example, both of which have strong, narrow, sword-shaped foliage).

▷ Transferring: this refers to flowers that project over the foliage on the end of long stalks, such as ornamental allium and globe thistles. These can be arranged to float over herbaceous perennials creating points of colour.

*Below left: The shapes and colours of these late summer flowers complement each other perfectly: ox eye (*Heliopsis helianthoides var. scabra*) and culver's root (*Veronicastrum virginicum 'Album'*). Below right: Peony (*Paeonia*), Salvia nemorosa and knautia (*Knautia macedonica*) master the interplay between flowers of different shapes and sizes.*

What does 'texture' mean?

Although its meaning is disputed by many specialists and it lacks a clear definition, by being aware of the term 'texture' we can sharpen our perception of plants and to improve our ability to design with them. Texture is mainly used to categorize leaf characteristics and is often used to compare the sizes and internal subdivision of leaves. Leaf qualities can be divided into five levels of texture:

▷ Very coarse (eg false spiraea, *Astilboides tabularis*),

▷ Coarse (eg lady's mantle, *Alchemilla mollis*),

▷ Medium (eg common lilac, *Syringa vulgaris*),

▷ Fine (eg bushy aster, *Aster dumosus*),

▷ Very fine (eg fennel, *Foeniculum vulgare*).

Some people include flowers and form in texture, while others refer rather to the visual and tactile qualities of the surface of the foliage, for example shiny, dull, smooth, rough, velvety or coarse (see pages 84–85).

Restraint and subdued colouring produce a delicate interplay between the shapes of the plants and the leaves in this pond-side planting. Over the yellow flowery carpet of creeping Jenny (Lysimachia nummularia), round plantain lilies (Hosta), a funnel-shaped royal fern (Osmunda regalis), a simple narrowleaf burr reed (Sparganium emersum) – like an erect poker – and the elegant white lines of the Japanese irises (Iris laevigata 'Variegata') stretch up towards the light with their distinctive forms. The foliage creates a contrast like 'harps and kettledrums' in a confrontation between the sword-shaped iris foliage and the rounded leaves of primroses (Primula alpicola), water lilies and plantain lilies.

Using Colours

It is not at all surprising that colour wields the greatest
fascination in flowerbed design. Along with fragrance,
colours, their tones and hues, directly affect our emotions.
Experience of a wide variety of plants is invaluable when
using colour, as it enables you to create subtle, individual,
original compositions from the sensitive use of the effects
that arise from different plant combinations. Once you have
begun to investigate these effects, you will be keen to
experiment further. Quench your thirst for colour and have
courage in your own creativity!

A Brief Theory of Colour

The full palette of primary colours, yellow (Heliopsis helianthoides 'Mars' and Alchemilla mollis), red (Hemerocallis 'Top Priority' and H. 'Mallard' as well as Achillea 'Walter Funke') and blue (Delphinium), creates a heady scene, which, without the green foliage to form a link between them, would produce harsh and clashing contrasts. These splashes of colour are reminiscent of a cottage garden style.

Colours are visible light. The colours of plants are reflected light that is not absorbed by the plant tissue. Luckily, you can start to get to grips with this complicated, albeit fascinating subject by following a few straightforward guidelines.

The colour wheel

The primary colours are red, blue and yellow and are regarded as pure colours because they cannot be created by mixing other colours. All other colours and tones are created by mixing the primary colours. Lighter or darker shades are achieved by adding white or black, the so-called 'non-colours'.

Secondary colours are orange (from mixing yellow and red), purple (from blue and red) and green (from blue and yellow). Develop your colour theory by using a colour wheel, which puts the secondary colours between the relevant primary colours. Depending on the proportion of the mix, different nuances will be

obtained. Pastel colours can be made from all of these colours by adding white, increasing the range of the palette by introducing varying amounts. A similarly wide range of colours can also be achieved by shading with black.

Warm colours include yellow, orange and red and are situated on one side of the colour wheel. Blue, turquoise and green have a cooler effect and are situated on the opposite side of the colour wheel. Complementary colours are beside each other on the colour wheel while contrasting ones are opposite each other, for example red and green, blue and orange or yellow and violet are contrasts while blue and purple, red and orange and green and yellow are complementary. Although, in a garden context, green is usually complementary by virtue of its overwhelming presence.

The qualities of colours

Although the physical qualities of colours can be measured objectively, a gardener should not use them too rigidly. Just like an artist, we need to be aware of the effects of colour, using them as a source of inspiration.

▷ Flower and leaf colours vary according to texture. Shiny surfaces intensify colours while matt surfaces dampen them and make them appear lighter.

▷ Warm tones give a feeling of closeness and can make small gardens look even smaller.

▷ Cool tones, on the other hand, are visually subdued. Used in the background of small gardens, they will create the illusion of depth and make the garden appear larger.

▷ Colours in the garden also depend on the amount of light. Therefore, the location of the garden has to be taken into account. Sunlight displays strong colours to their best advantage, whereas pastel tones lose their fluidity in dazzling light. Their delicately romantic appearance is best developed in partial shade or under trees, from where they will radiate light. The weather (sunny or cloudy), the time of day and the seasons can also change the character of colours.

▷ Colours are above all influenced by their surroundings. Gertrude Jekyll (1843–1932), a self-taught artist, demonstrated that colour does not have an effect on its own but rather in combination with other colours. A dark border will make a flowerbed appear smaller and a light border will make it appear larger. One complementary colour will enhance the effects of another, especially when they are used in unequal quantities.

Design options

Like Gertrude Jekyll, William Robinson was in favour of harmonious combinations of colours. This is achieved with:

▷ single-coloured (monochrome) plantings

▷ colour-co-ordinated combinations, that is different shades of the same colour (colour values)

▷ flowerbeds with progressions of colour (ie with neighbouring colours from the colour wheel)

▷ as well as planting purely cool or warm colours together.

But if you prefer exciting, lively designs, try contrasting rich duos or trios of colour and tone down any strong colour clashes by using white, silver, grey or green. When next to intense colours, subtle colours will be lost unless they are used in large quantities.

In contrast to garish primary colours, soft pastel tones can be combined in a harmonious liaison, creating elegant displays as demonstrated here by milky bellflower (Campanula lactiflora 'Loddon Anna'), rose campion (Lychnis coronaria 'Alba') and astilbe (Astilbe arendsii 'Bressingham Beauty').

Green – From Accessory to Leading Role

Green is often seen as having a secondary role, mediating between clashing flower colours as a neutral part of a plant. This view is contested, however, in many gardens. Italian Renaissance gardens, English landscape gardens and Japanese gardens prove that green can be used as an independent colour to create delightful designs.

Leaves are coloured

Although green flowers do exist, the colour green is primarily associated with foliage. In green plantings, evergreen leafy shrubs, such as yew (*Taxus*), box (*Buxus*) or holly (*Ilex*), are particularly popular. Conifers, bedding plants and decorative leafy herbaceous perennials can provide decoration throughout the entire growing season. Together with grasses and ferns, they form the so-called structural plants that combine enduring attractive foliage with impressive leaf and growth forms.

If you do not want to dedicate an entire garden to the colour green, you can reserve sunny areas for colourful summer flowers and magnificent herbaceous perennials. Partially shaded and shady areas, however, are ideal sites for green displays; there is a large choice of plants with ornamental leaves, including many ferns that relish these conditions.

When a single colour, such as green, is used, all the other characteristics of the plants, such as form, texture and shape, come to the fore.

Tips for using green

▷ Green flowerbeds in front of a dark background, for example a yew hedge, are best in light green tones. Conversely, dark green should predominate in front of light green, such as a beech hedge.

▷ Due to their higher level of luminosity, light green plants are used in smaller quantities in combinations than mid- or dark green plants.

▷ In the same way, plants with coarse textures (with large rough leaves) should be used more sparingly than finely textured plants. They should also be avoided in small gardens or niches because of their strong visual impact.

Below left: *A planting is not only enlivened by different leaf shapes, the light will also lend all sorts of nuances to the green of the ostrich fern (*Matteuccia struthiopteris).

Below right: *Like mighty parasols, the large leaves of* Gunnera manicata, *which grow up to 2m (6ft 6in) across, tower over the flowers and foliage of the Japanese primrose (*Primula japonica). *Although the gunnera is extremely vigorous, it must be protected from frost throughout the winter. Both examples prove another point: the eye receives a double treat when green is combined with red or white, offering a welcome change, as illustrated here with sweet woodruff (*Galium odoratum).

To avoid monotony, large single-coloured flowerbeds should mix different shapes and heights. This planting of box, mounds of drooping common ivy (Hedera helix), hydrangea and cherry laurel (Prunus laurocerasus 'Caucasia') makes good use of mainly evergreen, unusually shaped shrubs.

▷ Plants with fine textures are not successful in flat plantings as they do not have a strong enough structure.

▷ The most harmonious plantings are those that contrast only one of the plant characteristics (such as colour tones, textures, shape and surface) and then vary it gently. As a rule, limit the number of tones of green and textures you use in one flowerbed.

▷ You can create exciting effects by combining

Decorative green and leafy herbaceous perennials
▷ Lady's mantle (*Alchemilla mollis*)
▷ Bergenia (*Bergenia* species/hybrids)
▷ Brunnera (*Brunnera macrophylla*)
▷ Barrenwort (*Epimedium* species/varieties)
▷ Plantain lilies (*Hosta* species/hybrids)
▷ Solomon's seal (*Polygonatum* species/hybrids)
▷ Rodgersia (*Rodgersia* species)

two or three plant properties but they should not cover large areas as this will produce a generally unsettling feeling.

Creating illusions with green
Warm green, very coarse or coarse textures and shiny surfaces appear to come forward in a planting, while blue-green, dark green and grey-green, fine to very fine textures and matt surfaces have a distancing effect. By grouping together plants with these characteristics you increase the effect. In order to give a small garden visual depth and spaciousness, use plants that generate a feeling of nearness in the foreground, and place plants with a distancing effect in the background. A long garden can be made to look shorter by reversing this principle.

White, Silver and Grey

White, silver and grey begin to glow in the half-light, when they reflect more light than they absorb. Nocturnal revellers and plant-lovers who only find time for the garden in the evening should therefore place these colours near to the seating area. These plants can also be combined together and are often classified as neutral colours that tone down clashes. This, however, may not always be the case.

White is not only white

White flowers can be made of pure white or they can have hints of other colours such as pale vanilla, pink, apricot, or maroon, which can be used to create different effects. Large pure white flowers, for example annual mallow (*Lavatera trimestris* 'Mont Blanc') or white cosmos (*Cosmos bipinnatus* 'Sonata White'), will accentuate the contrast between strong or gaudy neighbouring colours. Filigree and cloud-like flowers such as the flowering sea kale (*Crambe cordifolia*) and baby's breath (*Gypsophila paniculata*) have a different effect, mixing their transparency with all the colours of their environment.

Flowers in broken white will tend to help to soften transitions between other colours and harmonize better with stronger colours.

*In this bed of summer flowers, white cosmos (*Cosmos bipinnatus 'Sonata White'*) provides a strong and lively contrast to the cool colours of the dahlias ('Ted's Choice'), Verbena bonariensis, zinnia (Zinnia elegans 'Benary's Riesen Lila') and the flossflower (Ageratum houstonianum 'Blue Horizon').*

This design exudes harmony and romantic elegance. The only summer flowers used are the dahlia 'White Mark', amid the silver of the mealy sage (Salvia farinacea) and the green tones of the summer cypress (Bassia scoparia) and snow on the mountain (Euphorbia marginata).

White flowers look particularly enchanting in sunny flowerbeds when they are combined with delicate pastel tones and silvery-grey foliage or sprinkled between full colours. Yellow and white can also be charming, for example the yellow-white tulip 'Sweetheart' over the white rock cress (*Arabis caucasica*) or yellow roses over sweet alyssum (*Lobularia maritima*). Strong borders can be given rhythm and structure with large bunches of white (see photograph page 68). Most shade-loving perennials with small flowers and white leaf markings harmonize well with neighbouring plants and help to lighten dark areas of the garden at the same time.

Silver and grey for all occasions

Silver and grey leaves are the result of fine hairs or waxy deposits that protect the surface of the leaf from the wind and sun. All silver and grey-leafed plants are sun-worshippers and are able to mix with all colours under dazzling light. They complement warm tones such as yellow and orange (see photographs pages 64–65) as well as cool purples, pinks and blues. Mixed together, they also offer a rich variety of combinations, from woolly-white mats of lamb's ears (*Stachys byzantina*) to blue-grey or greenish-grey. A selection of these plants can be found in the table on pages 132–133.

Single-colour Planting

Above left: Globe thistle (Echinops ritro 'Veitch's Blue'), monkshood (Aconitum x cammarum 'Franz Marc') and long-leaved speedwell (Veronica longifolia 'Lila Karina') vie with their blue spheres, spikes and lobed foliage in a summery perennial flowerbed.
Above right: Annual flowering magic with red dahlias ('Ted's Choice') and delicate pink cosmos (Cosmos bipinnatus) surrounded by the decorative violet hue of Verbena bonariensis.

Monochrome plantings are man-made creations that can be even more stunning than nature itself. That is what makes them so attractive. Moreover, the uniform colour accentuates the shapes and textures of the plants. To be successful the height, form, flowering times, shapes and colours of the flowers and the characteristics of the leaves all need to be carefully co-ordinated.

White flowerbeds

In these ethereal and elegant plantings, foliage plays an important role. The more green takes hold in white settings, the more lively the flowerbed will appear. Silver and grey leaves or red and brown foliage tones will also contribute to the character of the flowerbed. White-variegated shrubs can be used to form a charming backdrop. Use the variegated creeper *Euonymus fortunei* 'Silver Queen', shrubs with silvery foliage such as the willow-leaved pear

(*Pyrus salicifolia*), then add the dark evergreen of yew (*Taxus*) or try shrubs with white flowers, such as those of the common lilac (*Syringa vulgaris*) or snowball tree (*Viburnum*). Finally, bring in a few touches of yellowish-green, violet or blue to really enliven the white colour scheme.

Blue flowerbeds

With their cool tones, blue gardens have an aura of tranquillity which is heightened by grey or bluish-green foliage. Watery light blue, deep violet and aubergine also play important roles. Use any of the wide variety of blue clematis to give extra height to the bed. Gertrude Jekyll pointed out that in such gardens it is not just a question of using blue flowers but rather the effect of the blue beside everything else. She suggested introducing white, cream or yellow in blue flowerbeds to give the muted composition a refreshing stimulus. The yellowish-green foliage of lady's mantle (*Alchemilla mollis*), gold-variegated *Euonymus fortunei* 'Emerald 'n' Gold', *Spiraea japonica* 'Goldflame', plantain lilies (*Hosta*) and grasses can also bring extra verve to blue plantings. However, if you want to maintain a more subdued atmosphere, use pink or lilac tones instead.

Red flowerbeds

Red can develop surprisingly different moods, depending on whether it is presented as a warm-toned scarlet-red or cool purple-red. Although warm and cool tones often combine to form striking scenes, it is best to avoid these combinations within one colour to be on the safe side. Colour combinations using contrasting intermediate colours of the same tone (for example yellow-red with violet-red) will often clash uncomfortably.

Flowerbeds in cool red can appear anything from restrained to extravagant to lyrical. Carmine, crimson and violet-red are wonderful combined with flowers in pastel tones or foliage in shades of grey, silver, black and brown. Ideal plants to use include red valerian (*Centranthus ruber*) and orpine (*Sedum telephium*) or ice plant (*Sedum spectabile*), whose powdery and dusty tones can be subordinated or artistically blended with dabs of blue-violet into impressionistic compositions.

At the foot of Buddleja davidii *'White Profusion' and* Hydrangea macrophylla *'Lanarth White', the white flowers of the windflower (*Anemone x hybrida *'Honorine Jobert') and the rose campion (*Lychnis coronaria *'Alba') frolic in the white flowerbed with the yellowish-green foliage of lady's mantle (*Alchemilla mollis) *and the silver-grey of the common rue (*Ruta graveolens) *and the silver speedwell (*Veronica spicata ssp. incana).

This planting mimics a place in the sun with its warm and cool yellows. Under the floral canopy of golden rain (Laburnum), the grey-leaved perennial beauty yellow asphodel (Asphodeline lutea) and frost-sensitive greenish-yellow Mediterranean spurge (Euphorbia characias ssp. wulfenii) jostle for favour with the violet iris (Iris barbata hybrid).

Flowerbeds in warm red colours, on the other hand, draw attention to themselves with their loud and fiery character. Flower colours in the brick red and vermilion of the red hot poker (*Kniphofia*) and montbretia (*Crocosmia*) are matched by many annuals such as nasturtium (*Tropaeolum*), brilliant lobelia (*Lobelia fulgens*) or zinnia. One classic is the dahlia Bishop of Llandaff. Rust and copper tones help to provide other areas of interest in the flowerbed and add a calming influence, for example the black-brown or bronze-coloured foliage of *Heuchera micrantha* var. *diversifolia* 'Palace Purple' or red barberry (*Berberis thunbergii*). Scarlet goes very well with an accompaniment of yellow-green, the two making a dazzling combination. Chose

shrubs with good foliage colours to renew the lost summer glow of the flowerbed with their fiery autumn colouring.

Yellow flowerbeds

Bright and sunny, yellow flowerbeds always appear larger than they really are, seemingly pushing themselves forward into the centre of attention. Warm, sunny, yellow tones, together with cool lemon or sulphur-yellow, white or silver, can provide a heady progression of colours. While warm, yellow saturated flowerbeds can be broken up with small patches of orange and brown or white and silver, they can also be combined with blue and violet to create strong contrasts.

Colour Combinations

Just as too many elements give a bewildering and overcrowded appearance, especially in a smaller garden, using too many colours also has a disturbing effect. As we have already seen, single-coloured flowerbeds are anything but dull. However, many of us prefer to combine a number of colours. It is best to limit any colour combination to a maximum of four different colours, one of which should be white, silver, grey or reddish-brown – flowerbeds are enriched by lightened and darkened tones and generally are most pleasing to look at. Multicoloured beds are achieved not only by using flowers with the same blooming time but also by linking flower and leaf colours, which, depending on the focal point, can appear multilayered. With care, multicoloured beds can also be created using only leaf colours, such as yellow-green, violet-green, red-brown, grey or silver, as well as yellow or white variegated foliage, and these can be very effective.

Colours in groups

Before choosing any plants, try to visualize the effect you are hoping to achieve. The location of the flowerbed and the level of light it receives will also contribute to the overall appearance of the colours. In full sunshine, flowers with deep and dark tones do not lose any of their strength whereas the dim light of partial shade is more suited to enhancing light pastel tones.

▷ Combinations of pastel shades or similar colours have a harmonious effect.

▷ Group compositions with contrast and energy are created by designing with full tones of primary or complementary colours.

Any colour combination will also be affected by the size of the flowerbed and the proportions of each of the colours used. The larger the group of plants, the more clearly it will stand out against its neighbours and retain its individual character. While small areas of colour can be used to highlight certain spots, they will

Below left: *In the sunshine, the cypress spurge (Euphorbia cyparissus) appears to glow from the inside out. The violet globes of the ornamental onion (Allium aflatunense) liven up the planting and make it more three-dimensional.*
Below right: *Similar colours, but what a difference in atmosphere! In the partial shade, yellow is integrated with green so that lady's mantle (Alchemilla mollis), plantain lilies (Hosta fortunei 'Gold Standard') and Turkish sage (Phlomis russeliana) stand out against the purple penstemon.*

Herbaceous perennials and summer flowers are not the only source of colour. Here a sleek duo of climbing plants soars into the air: shining blue clematis 'Perle d'Azur' and fragrant white wisteria (Wisteria floribunda 'Alba').

Stunning vitality is created in this three-coloured bed of summer flowers by the rich tones of the yellow sunflowers (Helianthus annuus) *and marigolds, the red of the brilliant lobelia (*Lobelia fulgens)*, and the white petunias and mini Marguerite (*Argyranthemum frutescens)*. This colourful spectacle is enhanced by using foliage with different textures and shapes.*

not be effective if all the colours are presented in equally small dabs.

The density of a colour and how heavily it can be used also depend on the size of the flowers and the intensity of their tones. Plants with large flowers and strong colours create striking coloured surfaces.

Large flowers of a single colour can also be interwoven to melt into an impressionist-style scene. This effect can also be achieved with:

▷ loosely structured inflorescences scattered on coloured backgrounds

▷ plants whose tiny flowers create a veil-like effect, for example *Verbena bonariensis*, baby's breath (*Gypsophila paniculata*) and loose, filigreed grasses

▷ plants in subdued colours.

Striking combinations of colours
▷ White + pastel tones (yellow, blue, red)
▷ Silvery foliage + white, pink, purple, violet
▷ White + pink + violet
▷ Yellow + blue (violet) (+ white, silvery grey)
▷ White + wine red (pink) + blue (light blue)
▷ Wine red + purple (violet) + mid-blue
▷ Orange + violet + yellow-green (+ rust brown)
▷ Scarlet + golden yellow + yellow-green (+ rust)

The overall effect of any two colours is also influenced by the positions of the flowers in relation to each other. Thus even the strong violet of a carpet of pansies has to give way to delicate pink tulips towering overhead. So height, too, can determine the relative status of a colour.

This cool, rich three-coloured contrast between red (mallow), blue (monkshood) and white (Hydrangea arborescens 'Annabelle') is charmingly tempered by the frothy pink of the rose.

In a grand gesture, spring spreads its cheerful charm with pinks, blues and yellows. The captivating blooms of the flowering dogwood (Cornus florida 'Rubra') look simply stunning in this vibrant environment.

Colour Harmonies

For the beginner, there is little more pleasing than creating a successful colour composition for the first time. Good combinations can be very soothing, both to the eye and the spirit, and it is wonderful to be able to sit and enjoy something that you have made by yourself.

Co-ordinated combinations

Co-ordinated plantings are based on different shades of a single colour, lightened with varying amounts of white or darkened with different amounts of black. Countless variations are possible and can be used to produce fine and discreet colour effects.

Colour progressions

Flowerbeds that are based on colour progression mostly function with three or four colours that are adjacent on the colour wheel, whether they are 'full' colours or pastels. The relationship between these colours can be arranged in different ways:
▷ The colour construction in the flowerbed can follow the colour wheel progression.
▷ The colours can be freely combined in different quantities, sizes and proportions, perhaps even arranged in waves.
▷ The colours can be used as part of a delicate style of planting, designing with myriad colours or with co-ordinated colours or progressions. For example, small quantities of annuals or bulbs can be mixed together or large numbers of a recurring leading colour can be interwoven.

Top left: With fine colour-co-ordination purple loosestrife (Lythrum salicaria), bergamot (Monarda hybrid) and phlox (Phlox paniculata hybrid) merge into a truly lyrical scene.
Middle left: A summery colour progression using the sunny tones of tickseed (Coreopsis verticillata), coneflower (Rudbeckia fulgida var. sullivantii), sneezeweed (Helenium hybrid) and ox eye (Heliopsis helianthoides subsp. scabra).
Bottom left: In late spring, columbines (Aquilegia hybrids) produce a colour-co-ordinated graduation from blue to violet.

A daring progression in colour from yellow, through orange and pink, ending up with cool red; the bulleyana primrose (Primula bulleyana hybrids) frolics over the white cranesbill (Geranium rivulare).

This impressive double
border is clearly the work
of an artist. White mullein
(Verbascum chaixii
'Album') and pearly
everlasting (Anaphalis
margaritacea) liven up the
flow from red to orange to
yellow. Plume poppy
(Macleaya microcarpa),
with its loose copper-
coloured panicles, towers
above the floral sea of
sunny colours punctuated
by the rich orange notes of
Peruvian lily (Alstroemeria
Ligtu hybrids). Allowing
colours and nuances to
mingle together rather
than planting in blocks, has
resulted in a very natural
effect.

Colourful Accessories

Decorative garden accessories lend the finishing visual touches to the bed, shaping it with their style – classical, romantic or modern. Accessories also allow you to:

▷ fill an empty area or breathe colour into a green bed

▷ create new combinations of colours without using flowers

▷ disguise a weak spot in the garden or hide an unattractive one.

In order to achieve these results, accessories do not necessarily have to be brightly coloured. The material, for example wood, natural stone, terracotta, rust-encrusted metal or reflective glass, as well as their shape also contribute to the overall impression.

To add height

As well as evergreen shrubs in cone and column shapes, use long-stemmed plants, statues and sculptures, vases, plinths with urns or bowls on top to add a touch of vertical splendour. Any of these elements can make striking features that will extend the harmony and contrast of colour during flowering times or become the centre of attention during flowerless periods.

'Emergency plants'

You can avoid a lack of colour in flowerbeds with the help of 'emergency plants'. Gertrude Jekyll always kept a small army of young plants at the ready to fill in gaps in flowerbeds or to

The earthy rust colour of this bird bath transforms it into an artistic feature in a shady flowerbed. It is surrounded by Kirengeshoma palmata, pink-flowering meadow rue (Thalictrum aquilegifolium), golden shield fern (Dryopteris affinis), rodgersia (Rodgersia pinnata 'Elegans'), hydrangea (Hydrangea aspera) and meadowsweet (Filipendula purpurea 'Elegans'), and its base is swathed in plantain lilies (Hosta 'Undulata') and yellow corydalis (Corydalis lutea).

Above: *Over a cloud of fleabane (*Erigeron karvinskianus*), this cherub, releases a light violet flare of petunias.*
Right: *Instead of a flowerbed, a small container garden rings the changes in this quiet corner. It is not only its positioning that is enchanting but also the sky-blue tone of the table, which echoes the colours of the plants in the pots.*

break up an unsuccessful combination, inserting them as replacements or reinforcements. Emergency plants can also come in useful when they are used in containers that can then be sited in various places around the garden to brighten up a dull spot, or provide interest once the main season is over or before it begins. You could make these gaps part of the design as a permanent winter 'empty spot' for frost-sensitive beauties to occupy from spring to autumn, for example New Zealand flax (*Phormium tenax*).

Games with colours

Colourful accessories can create a constant visual effect from spring to autumn against the changes in the colours of the flowers. Accessories can turn monochrome flowerbeds into a combination of colours, especially when distributed throughout the bed. They can also add missing colours or balance out uneven colouring. Colourful and bright objects also help to enliven a green, shady planting.

Designing for Colour
all the Year Round

To have flowers year round demands an extensive
knowledge of plants, and so beginners should start with less
ambitious goals. Flowerbeds that have only one or two main
periods of bloom are ideal, for example spring (left-hand
page) and autumn (above). You could plant up a number of
flowerbeds that will each be transformed into islands of
floral delight at different times to enhance different areas of
the garden. Near patios and seating areas, however, a
constantly colourful scene is more important and can be
easily achieved with the help of colourful foliage.

Spring Magic

Spring raises its head in front of and under leafy shrubs with delightful bulb and tuberous plants such as snowdrops, spring snowflakes, early crocuses and cyclamens. Although they thrive in flowerbeds, they will be equally magnificent when allowed to naturalize in a shrub border, on a bank or in a meadow. Crocuses and many narcissi can also be freely planted in the lawn. However, the large-flowered hybrid varieties of tulips and daffodils belong in the flowerbed.

Plant tips

▷ The more decorative the spring blooms, the more important it is to plant them in swathes and drifted groups.

▷ After flowering, the foliage of bulb flowers gradually becomes less attractive so they should be placed in the middle of the flowerbed where they are concealed by the emerging shoots of the plants in front of them.

▷ Late spring herbaceous perennials that die back early and leave behind gaps in the flowerbed, such as bleeding heart (*Dicentra spectabilis*) or oriental poppy (*Papaver orientale*), should also be placed in the middle area of the flowerbed for the same reason.

▷ With their stiff form, tulips and daffodils appear more graceful when linked with biennial flowers such as pansies (*Viola* x *wittrockiana*), bellis (*Bellis*) or forget-me-nots (*Myosotis*), whose pink and white varieties further increase the number of potential combinations.

▷ Spring-flowering cushion perennials are best placed in the foreground where evergreens, such as aubretia (*Aubrieta* hybrids), perennial candytuft (*Iberis sempervirens*) or gold dust (*Aurinia saxatilis*), will remain handsome after their flowering period. In subdued colour compositions, the intense sunny yellow of the gold dust is particularly effective.

Below left: *As if they were made for each other, 'Orange Emperor' tulips and 'Fortissimo' daffodils, whose inner corona echoes the orange tulips.*
Below right: *Cool tones. The 'Blue Heron' tulip dances over the forget-me-nots (*Myosotis*) and blue pansies (*Viola* x *wittrockiana* hybrids).*
Right-hand page: *The white of the fragrant snowball (*Viburnum* x carlcephalum*) and perennial candytuft (*Iberis sempervirens*) complements the yellow daffodils and the orange tulips, creating a cheerful trio of colours.*

Summer Dreams

If you want to create a densely flowering bed, you must decide when it is going to reach its magical climax – in early, mid- or late summer. Next select the leading and accompanying plants, along with filling plants to extend the blooming time.

▷ Important leading plants for early summer to midsummer are roses, delphiniums, irises and peonies. To go with these, choose a number of plants that have a certain amount of permanent appeal, such as lady's mantle (*Alchemilla mollis*), catmint (*Nepeta* x *faassenii*), red valerian (*Centranthus ruber*) and bellflowers (*Campanula*), so you prolong the flowering period.

▷ Leading herbaceous perennials that excel in midsummer to late summer include perennial phlox (*Phlox paniculata* hybrids), bergamot (*Monarda*), foxgloves (*Digitalis*), day lilies (*Hemerocallis*), ligularias, desert candles (*Eremurus*) and mullein (*Verbascum*). Good accompanists with a wide range of varieties are fleabane (*Erigeron* hybrids), perennial flax (*Linum perenne*), sage (*Salvia nemorosa* and others) and sneezeweed (*Achillea ptarmica*).

▷ Important late-summer/early-autumn leading herbaceous perennials include purple loosestrife (*Lythrum salicaria*), golden rod (*Solidago* hybrids) and other sun-lovers such as ox eye (*Heliopsis helianthoides* var. *scabra*) or perennial sunflowers (*Helianthus decapetalus*), dahlias, montbretia and red hot pokers (*Kniphofia*), which can be charming accompanied by yarrow (*Achillea* hybrids), globe thistles (*Echinops*) or long-leaved speedwell (*Veronica longifolia*).

Autumn Atmosphere

Even though the flowers of many midsummer perennials have begun to fade away, gardens in the next month or two do not have to be lacking in colour. Shrubs with colourful foliage can now take on responsibility for a spectacular display in the garden and can be given vital support by impressive ornamental grasses. The desire for autumn blooms, however, can also be fulfilled. Many summer perennials, and bulb and tuberous plants that are planted a bit later, for example dahlias, gladioli, montbretia (*Crocosmia*), summer hyacinths (*Galtonia candicans*) and elegant gladioli (*Gladiolus callianthus*), will give a late floral display, providing a seamless transition into autumn. Other plants that are only now just beginning to show their most attractive side should be carefully matched with the autumn colouring of the shrubs.

Late-blooming magic

The second flush of the delphinium shines with an intense blue, as do, even more so, the robust autumn monkshood (*Aconitum carmichaelii*) and aromatic subshrubs such as bluebeard (*Caryopteris* x *clandonensis*) and Russian sage (*Perovskia*), attracting bees to a late celebration of flowers. The second flowering of roses, along with the red-coloured umbels of orpine (*Sedum*

*This brilliant autumn border comes to life with the parchment tones of the grasses and the burgundy red of the herbaceous perennials. In front of the backdrop of hemp agrimony (*Eupatorium fistulosum*), Chinese silver grass (*Miscanthus sinensis 'Malepartus'*) and willowherb (*Epilobium angustifolium*), large groups of plantain lilies (*Hosta*), gossamer-like purple love grass (*Eragrostis spectabilis*), bistort (*Persicaria amplexicaulis*) and grey-green hard fescue (*Festuca cinerea*) luxuriate.*

Here, colour is distributed over large areas and in a graduated progression. The wide, spreading violet of the dark Michaelmas daisy (Aster novi-belgii) and Aster ericoides is supported by the tall structures of the feathered reed grass (Calamagrostis x acutiflora 'Karl Foerster') and the fluttering silver pampas grass (Cortaderia selloana). The flowerbed is crowned by the red of the shrubs in the background.

telephium), ice plant (*S. spectabile*) and the small flowering clouds of the lesser calamint (*Calamintha nepeta*), also provide a tantalizing treat. But what would autumn be without the asters, which provide the entire repertoire of cool colours! Tall-growing plants such as *Aster laevis*, New England aster (*Aster novae-angliae*) and Michaelmas daisies (*Aster novi-belgii*) now assume a leading role or liven up the background of an autumn flowerbed. The low-growing counterparts, such as the dwarf *Aster sedifolius* 'Nanus' or bushy aster (*Aster dumosus* hybrids), hold their ground at the front. Partially shaded areas, on the other hand, are perfect for late-flowering anemones (*Anemone hupehensis* and *A. x hybrida* varieties).

Grasses for autumn flowerbeds

Ornamental grasses can look extremely elegant in flowerbeds. In autumn, many shine in corn-yellow or reddish colours, or powerfully assert their presence, like the pampas grass (*Cortaderia selloana*), with its feathery brush-like panicles up to 50cm (20in) long.

Grasses with divine autumn colouring

▷ Chinese fountain grass (*Pennisetum alopecuroides*)
▷ Chinese silver grass (*Miscanthus sinensis*, many varieties)
▷ Feathered reed grass (*Calamagrostis* × *acutiflora* 'Karl Foerster')
▷ Purple moor grass (*Molinia arundinacea*, *M. caerulea*)
▷ Silver spear grass (*Achnatherum calamagrostis*)
▷ Switch grass (*Panicum virgatum*, many varieties)

Winter Ornament

This charming winter flowerbed clearly demonstrates what can be achieved using the structure of plants. Different varieties of Chinese silver grass (Miscanthus sinensis), poker-straight reed grass (Achnatherum calamagrostis 'Karl Foerster'), pampas grass (Cortaderia selloana) with its feathery sensations and the long brushes of the Chinese fountain grass (Pennisetum alopecuroides) attest to the success of this winter arrangement.

In the winter, the garden changes from a place of sensory delights into an enchanting vision to be admired from the comfort of the house. The view from indoors at least should be aesthetically pleasing. The trusty basics of colour and structure in the form of frost-resistant garden ornaments, shrubs and grasses continue to bring interest. Evergreen and enduring herbaceous perennials left uncut after their flowers have faded can look truly inspiring when they become 'sugar-coated' in crystalline hoar frost and snowflakes.

Winter 'place holders'

The dormant period of the garden is lengthy and will reveal whether the structure and the distribution of the colours of the evergreen shrubs is well balanced. While formal flowerbeds sparkle and have a lofty air when outlined in hoar frost, informal flowerbeds can also generate subtle winter scenes using:

▷ evergreen herbaceous perennials such as bergenias, Christmas rose and tall bearded iris
▷ evergreen shrubs such as rhododendrons, lily of the valley bush and cherry laurel
▷ evergreen and faded grasses
▷ seed heads of long-lasting herbaceous perennials, such as orpine (*Sedum telephium*), Turkish sage (*Phlomis russeliana*), giant angelica (*Angelica gigas*), Chinese lanterns (*Physalis alkekengi* var. *franchetii*), common teasel (*Dipsacus sylvestris*), eryngo (*Eryngium*) or globe thistles (*Echinops*)
▷ coloured shoots and leaves, such as the red of the Siberian dogwood (*Cornus alba* 'Sibirica').

Continuously Colourful Flowerbeds

Flowerbeds that delight both heart and eye with a continuous display from the first awakenings of spring to the onset of the following winter are among the most ambitious of the gardener's desires. Flowering plants, however, are as delicate and mortal as we humans and generally flower only once a year for a short time. A continuously flowering border will place high demands on planning and design if you do not want to keep changing the plants. Even then, herbaceous perennials must be present in the flowerbed at all times, and their contribution is not so much made with their flowers but rather with the colours and shapes of their foliage. When you start making your plans, it will soon become apparent that it is considerably easier to achieve the impression of permanent flowering in big flowerbed which has the space to include lots of plants. In small gardens, however, in which all the beds are close together and the need for continuous blooms is often at its greatest, large borders are not always the best solution.

Year-round flowers in small beds

With flowerbeds of any size, it is useful for beginners to start with autumn and winter, the most difficult season, and then to work backwards to complete the design. So the big question is: what will bring colour in autumn, structure in winter and yet take up little space?

Around late spring, the crab apple (Malus toringo) makes a bold display with its foaming flowers. The mixed planting is defined by the evergreen shapes of the shrubs and subshrubs, such as Santolina rosmariniifolia and hebe (Hebe), which are permanent contributors to the flowerbed.

Just one of many possibilities is a box sphere as these maintain their shape and colour throughout the seasons. This basic shape could then be combined with an autumn planting that also has a dash of winter appeal. For example: Chinese fountain grass (*Pennisetum alopecuroides*) with red-flowering orpine (*Sedum telephium*), the silvery foliage of the wormwood (*Artemisia* 'Powis Castle') or lamb's ears (*Stachys byzantina*) and the violet flowers of the tall *Verbena bonariensis* or the lower-growing and denser bushy aster (*Aster dumosus* hybrids) – all will look good into the winter.

Annuals can be used throughout the summer to provide long periods of colour. They are cleared

from the flowerbed in the autumn to make room for spring-flowering plant bulbs, such as dwarf narcissi or crocuses, whose foliage quickly fades, or tulips, which are removed from the bed after they have flowered in order to plant summer flowers. There you have it – colour all year.

In early summer, herbaceous perennials are abundant and colourful, taking command of the flowerbed. The attractive small-leaved oleaster (Elaeagnus angustifolia) on the right-hand side of the picture launches a silver-leaved phase with its white felted foliage.

Preliminary decisions and plant selection

Planning a successful continuously blooming border can take all winter. Even Gertrude Jekyll puzzled at length over subtle combinations that were by no means based on inspiration alone. The first step to creating continuously flowering borders involves establishing the following points:

▷ Size and shape of the flowerbed

▷ Colours or combinations of colours at the various flowering times

▷ Construction (ascending or flat), structure and rhythm of the border.

The final stage is the selection of the plants. Any plants that might not give of their best should be discounted immediately.

Making use of seasonal building blocks

So as not to lose sight of the overall picture, make sure you establish a seasonal combination of leading plants, accompanying plants and filling plants for each flowering phase. These should meet your requirements for colour, height, form and shape of flower. Then using just a single plan, you can repeat these building blocks of spring, early summer, midsummer, late summer and autumn in varying quantities and in different combination to create seasonal themes of colour and shape.

To give the design a strong element of cohesion, place evergreen shrubs, grasses, colourful mediators, roses or plants in between your main

In autumn, the silver-grey and red of the orpine (Sedum) delight the eye as does the the golden yellow of the katsura tree (Cercidiphyllum japonicum).

Turning full circle. While the flowerbed is deep in the depths of winter slumber, the garden still benefits from the structure, shapes and colours of the shrubs.

grouping. They will then fill the beds for the otherwise flowerless periods of the planting. Once you have made a list, go back and check how each of the plants in your selection grow. Their habits should be taken into account to ensure that vigorous plants do not overgrow and crowd out their neighbours too quickly.

While the principle of interlocking seasonal flowering building blocks is rather theoretical it does constitute a solid starting point from which you can explore further possibilities. As you continue to garden you will gain experience and this will bring with it more ambitions and better ideas. You are therefore strongly advised to allow yourself the freedom to discard ideas that promised so much at one time but cannot satisfactorily be put into practice. Never be scared to dig up and move plants that do not work where they are.

Helpful tips

If there are gaps or other eyesores in the flowerbed, remember Gertrude Jekyll's 'emergency plants' and fill the space with pre-grown annuals from the nursery or correct the problem area with an attractive, matching potted plant or garden accessory. Try to choose plants with a long flowering period so they will go on into the next phase. For example, the flowers of the giant Persian allium (*Allium aflatunense*) will bridge the gap between late tulips and peonies, roses and delphiniums and, on a practical note, it is said to fend off moles and repel insects.

Always be ready to try new things and borrow other people's ideas, too: novelty can find its way into the border through inspiration from existing gardens or your own ideas and experiments. As the old adage goes, the road to discovery is half the fun!

Plants with long flowering times

▷ Lesser calamint (*Calamintha nepeta*)

▷ Red valerian (*Centranthus ruber*)

▷ Dahlia (*Dahlia*)

▷ Gaura (*Gaura lindheimeri*)

▷ Day lily (*Hemerocallis* hybrids)

▷ Catmint (*Nepeta* x *faassenii*)

▷ Cape fuchsia (*Phygelius capensis*)

▷ Coneflower (*Rudbeckia fulgida*)

▷ Salvia (*Salvia nemorosa*)

PRACTICAL GUIDE

Putting Theory Into Practice

Preparing the Ground

When setting out a new flowerbed, first of all establish and precisely mark out the size and shape of the bed. It is advisable to outline the location and shape of the bed with a hosepipe, thick cord or a measuring tape so as to check the visual effect of its shape and proportions from several sides, correcting it where necessary. This applies in particular to flowerbeds with freely sweeping contours, corner plantings or arrangements that divide up the garden like islands or partitions. Once you have completed this stage, you can begin to prepare the soil.

The importance of location

Whether alongside shrubs or at the edge of a pond, whether they contain herbaceous perennials or roses, flowerbeds need to provide for all the requirements of all their resident plants for the whole course of the year. Even the most robust cultivated plants will often have similar requirements – in terms of light, soil and moisture – as those of their wild forefathers, and plantings in flowerbeds will only develop their full potential under the right conditions.

In wild and natural flowerbeds the choice of plants must be governed by the existing light, soil and moisture levels. If you are buying plants from a good garden centre or nursery, the labels should provide information on what they need, or you can ask a member of staff.

Here are some tips on choosing plants that will thrive in your garden conditions:

▷ Herbaceous perennials from woodland environments prefer shade or partial shade as well as loose, often slightly moist soils with a high humus content.

▷ Herbaceous perennials that come from open locations and many rock garden perennials flourish in poor, dry, free-draining soil in full sunshine. Silver and grey-leaved subshrubs and herbaceous perennials feel particularly at home here.

▷ Herbaceous perennials from waterside and marshy environments tolerate or even revel in permanently waterlogged conditions.

Most herbaceous perennials and annuals as well as many herbs and vegetables prefer a sunny protected spot and well-prepared soil. The soil should be loose, fine and crumbly, contain humus and not be too wet. Many plants are happiest in slightly acidic soil with a pH value of 6–7, although it is possible to find plenty that will thrive in more alkaline conditions.

To avoid losing huge numbers of plants, choose those that like the soil conditions in your garden. For example, it is no good buying rhododendrons and camellias if you are on chalky alkaline soil – they simply will not thrive. You could grow them in a raised bed or in a container, if you really wanted to have them, but they will never look as if they belong.

There are a number of herbaceous perennials that are quite flexible about where they are grown: some plants which really love partial shade, such as lady's mantle (*Alchemilla mollis*), will also flourish in sunny flowerbeds if the soil supplies them with enough moisture to compensate. It is a matter of experience, having a look at what is growing in other people's gardens in your area and reading a good plant directory.

Step-by-Step Flowerbed Design

Soil types and remedies for herbaceous perennials

Light, sandy soil
▷ Properties: Loose, well aerated, warms quickly, low in humus and nutrients, dries out quickly.
▷ Remedy: Add and work in quantities of well-rotted garden compost, horse manure and leaf mould if available. Before planting, if possible, sow a green manure. Mulching around the base of plants and any open areas, perhaps with chipped bark, is also recommended.

Heavy loam and clay soils
▷ Properties: Tendency towards being damp and heavy, poorly aerated, cold and lacking in humus.
▷ Remedy: Dig deep to break up the clumps. Increase permeability and humus level with coarse sand or fine grit, and work in well-rotted compost or leaf mould. Before planting, sow a green manure. Dig it in later.

Acidic soil
▷ Properties: Many plants flourish best in slightly acidic soil (a pH of 7 or below is termed acidic). If the pH level is too low, however, the intake of nutrients is hindered.
▷ Remedy: Thinly work in hydrated lime once or twice a year.

Chalky soil
▷ Properties: pH value over 7.5. The intake of iron and magnesium is reduced and many plants become stunted and the foliage becomes yellow (chlorosis).
▷ Remedy: Work in compost and peat.

Getting to know the soil. Anyone faced with a new location for a flowerbed or a new garden should take soil samples from several places. There are commercial laboratories that will analyse soil for acidity level and nutrient content and advise on care and fertilizers. However, gardeners can easily test the acidity content of the soil (pH value) themselves. Simple, proprietary kits are available at most good garden centres. The usual instruction is to mix some soil with distilled water and then test with a strip of the indicator paper or some powder.

Soil preparation. With new beds, remove the topsoil and dig down to break up the underlying earth. Then, depending on the soil composition, improve it with fertilizer or compost, or both. In extremely wet areas, it may be necessary to lay some sort of drainage.

After clearing out old plants, the soil may be rather tired. To give old flowerbeds a new lease of life, sow a green manure crop and turn it in before replanting so that the new plants have growing conditions full of fresh vitality. If you begin to do this in the spring, the new flowerbed can be planted in the autumn with spring-flowering bulbs and tubers.

Establish a planting plan. First of all, roughly define the structure and construction of the flowerbed (see pages 124–125). Establish the colour and shape, height and grouping of the plants.

Choosing plants. Be careful about your selection of plants. Take into account colours and shapes, as well as flowering times. If you are composing groups of leading perennials, accompanying plants and filling plants in single seasonal phases, you need to consider many different aspects simultaneously.

Layout of a mixed flowerbed

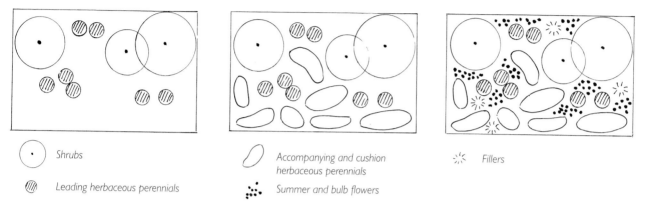

⊙ *Shrubs*

◍ *Leading herbaceous perennials*

⬭ *Accompanying and cushion herbaceous perennials*

⋰ *Summer and bulb flowers*

※ *Fillers*

1. Creating a framework for the flowerbed. Stagger and group shrubs in the background according to their flowering times or foliage colours. Ornamental shrubs or roses, for example, can emphasize or intensify the colours of the flowerbed by flowering at the same time. If you choose ornamental shrubs that reach their pinnacle (flowering time or autumn colouring) before or after the main flowering period of the flowerbed, you can extend the colour display into the autumn or even winter. Evergreen shrubs or small conifers, however, provide the flowerbed with constant structure throughout the winter.

2. Establish a highlight. This task naturally falls to the more domineering plants, the leading herbaceous perennials. Placed individually or in groups in the middle and background of the bed, they will determine its key colours, character and rhythm.

3. Accompanists and foreground. Low-growing perennials carry out their supportive role by surging around the leading herbaceous perennials in large groups, strengthening the sea of flowers with their colours and shapes by blooming at the same time. If you want to extend the flowering period of the flowerbed, choose accompanying plants with a particularly long flowering time or a later flowering time or one which will carry on into the next phase. Arrange them to flank the leading herbaceous perennials with their decorative foliage. The lowest-growing species come into play in the foreground. Evergreen cushion perennials that retain their shape after blooming are particularly effective alternated with perennials with decorative leaves or grasses that drape themselves over the edge of the flowerbed.

4. Prolong the flowering time. Place bulbs (such as tulips and narcissi) and early summer flowers (such as bleeding heart, Oriental poppy and globe flowers), which die back after blooming, in the middle and background so that the empty spaces they leave behind can be covered by the shoots of other plants. The same applies to inconspicuous annuals that only begin to display their full glory in early summer. Position low, autumn herbaceous perennials (such as bushy asters) in the foreground and high ones in the background where they slowly push upwards to radiate with passionate colours from early autumn onwards.

5. Improvements. If any 'gaps' threaten to spoil the composition, use perennial fillers or annuals to add any necessary touches of colour.

Group structuring of informal borders

These borders are characterized by having long band-like surfaces which contain mainly tall herbaceous perennials in narrow neighbouring groups in a graduated arrangement. These groups can assume completely different shapes and lend the border a wide variety of effects and patterns.

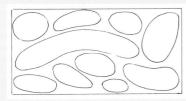

Different-sized drifts in a parallel graduated arrangement

Combination of drifts and circles that stand out as narrow columns or features

Diagonal drifts that create a wave-like appearance, giving the border a deep three-dimensional feel

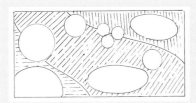

Carpet-like structures set against each other with small groups of accents and other features

Internal structuring of flowerbeds and borders

The patterns that can be used to plant a flowerbed or border are infinite. Think of the difference between a formal carpet-like flowerbed featuring monotone, geometric designs made with clearly defined colours and the impressionistic progression of an unstructured, modern, wild border and this will give you an idea of the vast range of design options. However it is best to avoid:

▷ Flowerbeds or borders with groups of plants of the same size
▷ Flowerbeds or borders with groups of the same shape
▷ Borders with plants of a uniform height.

Gardeners who are keen to experiment can juggle the following four criteria to create constantly changing garden scenes using:

The character of the plants: herbaceous perennials, annuals, roses and vegetables.

The size of the grouping: groups of the same size or different sizes.

The shape of the grouping: arrangements using unnatural or geometric patterns or natural shapes such as waves, irregular bands and ovals.

The perception of the flowerbed: view from the front and/or the sides.

If you mix herbaceous perennials of different sizes and character (for example imposing leading herbaceous perennials and accompanying perennials), the leading herbaceous perennials should be used in smaller quantities than their companions. The same plants or plants with an equivalent shape or colour should be repeated to create a rhythm at irregular intervals.

Examples of formal flowerbed construction with front access

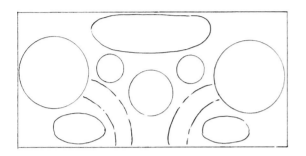

Large groups of plants in 'drifts' gradually draw the gaze towards the focal point at the back.

Yew columns and box spheres rise up on both sides of a flat carpet of roses and lavender.

Designing in drifts

Gertrude Jekyll described groups of ribbon-like plantings as drifts. There are two advantages to arranging plants in ribbon-like groups:

▷ Ribbons have a long section of contact with neighbouring groupings due to their long contours, allowing them to blend better.

▷ Depending on the course that they take, they will also provide the eye with a rich variety of impressions. If the drifts are parallel to the path, they will appear to draw together when viewed from the side, whereas when viewed from the front they will appear to run wide. If the drifts lie diagonally to the border, a rippling wave-like scene will be created (see photographs pages 72 and 110).

A diagonal arrangement was described by Jekyll as the ideal choice for a shady border under or in front of shrubs. She recommended planting ferns in diagonal drifts enclosed by an evergreen cushioning of *Saxifraga arendsii* hybrids at the edge of the border. Between the individual diagonals of the ferns, she placed bulbs and tubers from spring-flowering blooms in the following colour progression:

▷ pink: dog's tooth violets (*Erythronium*), cyclamen (*Cyclamen coum*), corydalis (*Corydalis*)

▷ through blue: windflower (*Anemone blanda*), Siberian squill (*Scilla sibirica*), grape hyacinth (*Muscari*), glory of the snow (*Chionodoxa luciliae*)

▷ and white: crocuses (*Crocus*) and hyacinths (*Hyacinthus*)

▷ to yellow: various wild narcissi (such as *Narcissus minor*).

After flowering, their wilting foliage will be covered by the freshly unfurling fronds of the ferns which will open up in summer with surges of green.

Designing from the front

If flowerbeds are placed at the end of a garden, line of sight or path and are therefore approached head on, they can be designed as a crowning finish with a central highlight, especially effective in formal gardens. For example, a statue, fountain or bench can be integrated into the flowerbed.

Planting, Care, Winter Protection

Planting tips

After planning the flowerbed and selecting flowers, it is important to purchase your plants in the right quantities. The box on the right is intended as a guideline. Before planting, break up and treat the soil in the flowerbed. It is important to remove all weed roots, such as ground elder, bindweed or horsetail, as once they have taken hold it is very difficult to get rid of them again especially from among your prized plants.

▷ Shrubs and herbaceous perennials are planted in the spring or autumn.

▷ Annuals are planted in late spring.

▷ Bulbs for spring flowers and lilies are planted in autumn.

▷ Bulbs and tubers of frost-sensitive flowers, such as dahlias and gladioli, are planted in early summer.

▷ Exceptions: The bulbs and tubers of crown imperial (*Fritillaria imperialis*), Madonna lily (*Lilium candidum*) and desert candle (*Eremurus* hybrids) are planted in late summer. In mixed flowerbeds, first plant roses and shrubs, doing it on an overcast day if possible. Herbaceous perennials can then be laid out around them; be prepared to move them about before deciding on their final positions. Then plant the flowerbed from back to front. Herbaceous perennials are planted as deeply in the soil as they were in their flowerpots. After planting, water all plants with a gentle spray of water and cover any bare surfaces with a mulch. This suppresses the growth of weeds and preserves the moisture in the soil.

Fertilizers

Wild herbaceous perennials in natural flowerbeds often require no fertilizer at all. In spring, however, bone meal can be worked into the soil. But some tall herbaceous perennials have higher requirements for nutrients. In the spring, they should be given compost and organic fertilizer

---

Purchasing guide: plants per square metre/yard

▷ Tall herbaceous perennials (1-2m/3-6½ft)   2-5 plants

▷ Medium-height herbaceous perennials (50-90cm/20-36in) and tall to medium-height summer flowers   5-9 plants

▷ Low-growing herbaceous perennials (20-40cm/8-16in) and summer flowers   7-12 plants

▷ Dwarf herbaceous perennials, bedding plants   10-16 plants

(depending on the soil type) that will slowly and gently take effect. Both are worked into the earth around the plants. Herbaceous perennials, roses and other shrubs should not be fertilized after late summer as the nitrogen in the fertilizer will stop the shoots from maturing, putting the hardiness of the plants at risk. Tall summer flowers can receive a liquid fertilizer once a month when they are watered, along with any container plants.

Summer care

Where soil is less than perfect, you will need to continue to improve it through the summer. Difficult soils need to be regularly broken up to prevent them from becoming muddy and crusty after rainfall (provided they have not been mulched). With slightly sandy soil, work in some well-rotted compost at intervals of four to six weeks so that the soil gets more humus and is more able to retain water. This type of soil also benefits from mulching. Wild herbaceous perennial plantings do not require this treatment.

Removing weeds is one of the most important jobs to be done throughout the summer on a regular basis. Hoe the weeds and remove them at the same time. They are most easily removed by hand if the soil is slightly moist.

Support. Tall garden flowers (such as tall asters) and herbaceous perennials with large heavy flowers (such as peonies) often need to be supported to prevent the wind and rain from snapping them, or their clusters from falling apart. If the ground is too rich in nutrients, herbaceous perennials can grow too lushly and too weakly and lose their strength. As one of the many aims of plant breeders is to produce more robust plants, it is worth taking note of this when selecting plants.

Individual tall plants, such as delphiniums or lilies, can be fixed to a garden cane. Drive a supporting cane deep into the ground and tie the plant loosely but firmly to the cane with a soft string. An additional decorative effect is created using stylish plant canes with decorated ends available from specialist shops. Ornamental canes blend beautifully with a sea of flowers.

For weak clusters, there are practical support systems available in various heights (for example link-stakes or similar) that can be adjusted to the surrounding plants.

Watering. Herbaceous perennials have varying water requirements. If the soil has dried out after a long hot spell, watering is necessary, preferably in the morning or evening with water that has been left to stand. A gentle drizzle from a watering can is the kindest and easiest method of watering and will avoid damage to the leaves or flowers.

Pruning. There are various reasons for cutting back shoots.

▷ Maintenance pruning involves removing the parts of plants that are dead or past their best. This will ensure that the flowerbed looks well cared for and prevents the plants from seeding too heavily. Removing dead or dying flowers will induce annuals and many herbaceous perennials to create new blooms, prolonging the overall flowering period.

▷ Second-bloom pruning is carried out on early summer herbaceous perennials, such as delphiniums (*Delphinium*), fleabane (*Erigeron*), lupins (*Lupinus*), knapweed (*Centaurea*), pyrethrum (*Tanacetum coccineum*), lady's mantle (*Alchemilla*

mollis) and many cranesbill (*Geranium*) varieties. If they are cut back to, say, 10cm (4in) above the soil after flowering, they will often flower for a second time in autumn.

▷ Rejuvenating pruning is necessary to maintain compact growth for dwarf shrubs such as lavender, Russian sage, common sage (*Salvia officinalis*), cotton lavender (*Santolina chamaecyparissus*), germander (*Teucrium*) and many cushion herbaceous perennials. After flowering, they are cut back by about a third.

▷ Overwintering. There are various views on hard-pruning herbaceous perennials before the onset of winter. Long lasting plants with pleasant seed heads (example page 112) and grasses can actually enrich the winter scene when enchantingly covered in hoar frost. They are best cut back in spring before the new growth begins.

Winter protection

Before the onset of winter, it is important to identify frost-resistant plants. Hardy herbaceous perennials require no winter protection at all, whereas more sensitive plants such as rodgersia (*Rodgersia*), bleeding heart (*Dicentra*), windflower (*Anemone hupehensis*) and plume poppy (*Macleaya*) need to be cut back in harsher climates and covered with foliage and brushwood. This should not be done too early but rather only when the temperature drops well below freezing so that the still-growing plants are not harmed.

▷ Evergreen herbaceous perennials can also be given a protective mulch.

▷ The leaves of yuccas and cordylines are loosely tied at the top to protect them and a protective mulch of foliage should be piled up around their base.

▷ The tubers of frost-sensitive plants such as dahlias and gladioli should be brought in and kept dry and frost-free in the greenhouse or shed over winter.

Fragrant Plants

Name	Height	Flowering time	Flowers	Situation	Notes
Fragrant shrubs					
Daphne mezereum Mezereon	1m (3ft)	late winter – mid-spring	pink-red	sunny to partially shady soil slightly moist, with humus, chalky	Red berry-like fruits from May; f. *alba* flowers white, var. *rubra* flowers red; all parts of the plant are highly poisonous.
Fothergilla major Mountina witch alder	2–3m (6½–10ft)	late spring	creamy white	sunny to partially shady soil with humus, slightly moist, acidic to neutral	Highly decorative, also suitable as a solitary plant; from late autumn magnificent golden-yellow to orange-red colouring.
Hamamelis hybrids Witch hazel	2–3m (6½–10ft)	winter	yellow, orange, bronze, copper, creamy white	sunny to partially shady soil with humus, permeable, neutral to acidic	Highly decorative, mainly suitable as a solitary plant; from late autumn magnificent golden-yellow to orange-red colouring.
Malus coronaria 'Charlottae' Wild sweet crab apple	5m (16ft)	late spring – early summer	delicate pink tufts	sunny to partially shady soil deep, chalky with humus	Large flowers up to 5cm (2in) diameter; from late summer green-yellow apples; orange-red autumn foliage.
Philadelphus hybrids Mock orange	1–3m (3–10ft)	late spring – early summer	white (double and single)	sunny to partially shady soil permeable, with humus	Very attractive with roses or lilac.
Rhododendron luteum Azalea	2m (6½ft)	late spring	golden yellow	sunny to partially shady soil permeable, with humus; up to pH value 6	Deciduous shrub; flowers appear in up to 12cm (5in) wide sweetly scented inflorescences before the leaves start to shoot; orange-red autumn colouring.
Rosa Bedding, shrub and climbing roses	0.4–3m (1½–10ft)	mid-spring – mid-autumn	white, yellow, salmon, orange, pink, red	sunny soil permeable, with humus; slightly loamy	For flowerbeds choose repeat-flowering varieties that are perfumed.
Syringa vulgaris hybrids Common lilac	4–6m (13–20ft)	late spring – early summer	white, pink, violet, purple, light yellow	sunny soil permeable, loamy, lime-loving	The pink-coloured *Syringa pubescens* ssp. *microphylla* 'Superba' has a sweet fragrance; flowers late summer to early autumn.
Viburnum farreri, *V. x bodnantense* 'Dawn' Fragrant viburnum, winter snowball	2–3m (6½–10ft)	winter – early spring	pink	sunny to partially shady soil permeable, with humus	Attractive autumn colouring; other species of snowballs, which flower in spring, also have a sweet fragrance.

Name	Height	Flowering time	Flowers	Situation	Notes
Fragrant herbaceous perennials					
Agastache foeniculum Anise hyssop	80cm (32in)	midsummer – mid-autumn	large violet panicles	sunny soil rich in nutrients, permeable, moderately moist	Herbaceous perennial with beautiful foliage and long flowering time; also white-flowering varieties: 'Album' and 'Alabaster'.
Aurinia saxatilis (formerly *Alyssum saxatile*) Gold dust	30cm (12in)	spring	rich yellow	sunny soil permeable, dry	Cushion-shaped subshrub; sulphur-yellow varieties 'Citrina' and 'Sulphureum' look good in combinations.
Calamintha nepeta Lesser calamint	40cm (16in)	late summer – late autumn	tiny delicate lilac flowers in large cymes	sunny soil permeable, dry	Enchanting with long flowering time; grows into clouds of bushes; goes well with roses and orpine (*Sedum telephium*).
Convallaria majalis Lily of the valley	25cm (10in)	late spring	white, bell shapes in clusters	partially shady to shady soil with humus, loose, slightly moist	Woodland plant, ideal in groups under shrubs and in front of walls; spreads rapidly using runners; all parts are poisonous.
Dianthus plumarius Feathered pink	20–30cm (8–12in)	late spring – midsummer	white, pink, red, also two-tone and double	sunny, warm soil permeable, sandy, rich in nutrients	Cushion plant with grey-green foliage; beautiful with lavender, sedum, summer savoury; also suitable for dry stone walls and rock gardens.
Dictamnus albus Burning bush	70cm (28in)	late spring – early summer	large, loose, candle-like pink clusters	sunny, warm soil permeable, stony, dry, chalky	Herbaceous perennial; beautiful with sage, speedwell, calamint, grasses; also ideal for rockeries.
Hemerocallis 'Baroni' Day lily	110cm (43in)	early summer – midsummer	light yellow, thin trumpet flowers	sunny to partially shady soil slightly moist, rich in nutrients, loamy	Some of the numerous hybrids are also fragrant; this variety begins to open up and release its fragrance in the evening.
Hosta species and hybrids Plantain lily	5–120cm (2–48in)	summer	white and violet- blue clusters	partially shady to shady soil slightly moist, with humus, loamy	Very decoratively leaved herbaceous perennial with charming leaf markings and shades of green as well as white and yellow-coloured leaves, many of which turn golden-yellow in autumn.
Iberis sempervirens Evergreen candytuft	20–30cm (8–12in)	mid-spring – late spring	white cymes	sunny soil permeable, low in humus, dry	Evergreen, cushion-like subshrub; for dry stone walls, rockeries and border foregrounds; beautiful with grasses (*Festuca*), tulips and painted leaf (*Euphorbia polychroma*).

Name	Height	Flowering time	Flowers	Situation	Notes
Fragrant herbaceous perennials					
Lavandula angustifolia Lavender	30–60cm (12–24in)	summer	blue-violet heads	sunny, warm soil dry, permeable, chalky, silty	Evergreen subshrub, also in white and pink varieties; classic companion for roses; can be combined in a variety of ways; very good in flowerbed borders.
Malva moschata Musk mallow	60cm (24in)	early summer – early autumn	single pink petals	sunny soil loose, with humus	Short-lived herbaceous perennial that seeds itself; the white variety 'Alba' is particularly beautiful; attractive in natural flowerbeds with grasses.
Monarda **hybrids** Bergamot	80–120cm (32–48in)	midsummer – early autumn	white, pink, red, violet-blue labiates	sunny, warm soil loose, slightly moist, rich in nutrients	Can assume the role of a leading herbaceous perennial; many colour combinations; leaves are also fragrant.
Nepeta x *faassenii* Catmint	20–60cm (8–24in)	early summer – early autumn	violet-blue panicles	sunny, warm soil permeable, dry, by no means heavy or wet	Can be combined and used in a great many ways; numerous varieties including white; 'Walkers Low' has large flowers and blooms for a long time.
Origanum vulgare Oregano	30–40cm (12–16in)	midsummer – early autumn	lilac-pink	sunny, warm soil loose, dry, rich in nutrients	'Compactum' has an especially compact habit; for rockeries, walls, sunny flowerbeds; beautiful with lavender, baby's breath (*Gypsophila*), pearly everlasting (*Anaphalis*).
Paeonia lactiflora **hybrids** Peony	80–100cm (32–39in)	late spring – early summer	red, pink, white, single and double	sunny to partially shady soil with humus, rich in nutrients, slightly moist	Leading herbaceous perennial with attractive leaves until late autumn; not all varieties are scented.
Persicaria wallichii Himalayan knotweed	1.5m (5ft)	early – mid-autumn	white panicles	sunny to partially shady soil with humus, rich in nutrients	Late flowers; good for wild areas in large gardens; can become invasive with rampant growth.
Primula vialii	30–60cm (12–24in)	early summer – midsummer	violet cone- shaped spikes	partially shady soil moist, but not waterlogged, with humus and rich in nutrients	Good in groups at the water's edge or by shrub borders and together with alum root, Himalayan poppies (*Meconopsis*), ferns and grasses; needs winter protection.
Salvia officinalis Common sage	30–60cm (12–24in)	early summer – midsummer	violet-blue heads	sunny, warm soil permeable, rich in nutrients, chalky	Aromatic subshrub; the varieties 'Purpurascens' with a purple colour, and 'Icterina' and 'Tricolor' with white, yellow and green foliage, are also decoratively leaved plants.

Name	Height	Flowering time	Flowers	Situation	Notes
Fragrant summer flowers					
Dianthus barbatus Sweet william	30–50cm (12–20in)	late spring – late summer	blue-violet heads	sunny soil permeable, slightly moist, rich in nutrients	Biennial; good cut flower; place in the middle of the flowerbed as the plants will leave gaps behind after they have flowered.
Dianthus caryophyllus Carnation	30–50cm (12–20in)	early summer – mid-autumn	single pink petals	sunny soil permeable, rich in nutrients	Annual; as well as low and tall-growing varieties there are also hanging carnations.
Erysimum cheiri Wallflower	30–60cm (12–24in)	mid-spring – early summer	white, pink, red, violet-blue labiates	sunny soil rich in nutrients, loamy, chalky	Biennial; there are tall varieties approx. 60cm (24in) tall and low varieties around 30cm (12in).
Hesperis matronalis Sweet rocket	60–100cm (24–39in)	late spring – early summer	violet-blue panicles	partially shady to shady soil permeable, rich in nutrients, chalky	Actually a wild herbaceous perennial but usually treated as a biennial; intoxicating evening fragrances; good in shady borders and natural-style gardens; the plants freely seed themselves.
Lathyrus odoratus Sweet peas	20–200cm (8–78in)	early summer – early autumn	lilac-pink	sunny to partially shady soil permeable, rich in nutrients, chalky	Annual; as well as climbing varieties there are also dwarf varieties that do not need staking for borders and medium-height varieties for flowerbeds.
Lobularia maritima Sweet alyssum	5–15cm (2–6in)	early summer – mid-autumn	red, pink, white, single and double	sunny soil permeable, not too rich in nutrients	Annual; charming continuous bloomer for a flowerbed border but also good between roses and in gaps in the foreground.
Lunaria annua Honesty	40–120cm (16–48in)	late spring – early summer	white panicles	sunny to partially shady soil with humus, slightly moist	Biennial; can be grown in an artistically wild manner at the edge of the shrub border between cranesbill and ferns; in the autumn, striking silvery seed heads – a must for flower arrangers.
Matthiola incana Brompton stock	30–90cm (12–36in)	early summer – early autumn	violet cone-shaped spikes	sunny soil with humus, slightly moist, rich in nutrients, chalky, not waterlogged	Annual; enchanting in groups with baby's breath or as filler plants.
Reseda odorata Mignonette	20–60cm (8–24in)	midsummer – early autumn	violet-blue heads	sunny to partially shady soil with humus, rich in nutrients, chalky	Annual; highly fragrant scent, especially bewitching in the evening.

Silver and Grey-leaved Plants

Name	Height	Flowering time	Flowers	Situation	Notes
Achillea 'Moonshine' Yarrow	60cm (24in)	summer	sulphur-yellow umbels on interwoven stems	sunny, warm soil permeable, dry, rich in nutrients	Robust herbaceous perennial with attractive silver foliage; the large flower heads have slightly darker disc-florets.
Anaphalis triplinervis Pearly everlasting	25–40cm (10–16in)	midsummer – early autumn	tiny silvery-white heads in umbrella-like clusters	sunny, hot soil permeable	Easily maintained herbaceous perennial; good with bushy asters (*Aster dumosus*), sage (*Salvia*) and grasses (*Festuca, Pennisetum*).
Artemisia absinthium 'Lambrook Silver' Wormwood	70cm (28in)	midsummer – early autumn	small, yellow, unassuming	sunny soil permeable, dry	Grey-green herbaceous perennial with finely cut leaves which over time becomes woody at the base; completely hardy.
Artemisia 'Powis Castle' Wormwood	50cm (20in)	midsummer – early autumn	small, yellow, unassuming	sunny soil permeable, dry	Grey-green, exceptionally finely textured foliage; the opulent bushes are also suitable for the foreground; do not prune until spring and give winter protection.
Artemisia ludoviciana 'Silver Queen' Wormwood	70cm (28in)	summer	yellowish, unassuming	sunny soil permeable, dry	Long silvery leaves; this strongly growing perennial has a tendency to crowd out other plants so only use in large flowerbeds.
Artemisia schmidtiana 'Nana' Wormwood	25cm (10in)	early summer – midsummer	white, unassuming	sunny soil permeable, sandy, dry, no water	Fine silvery foliage in tightly rounded bunches that will spread out over time; good in the foreground of the bed.
Artemisia vallesiaca Wormwood	40cm (16in)	late summer – early autumn	small yellow flowers with panicles of inflorescences	sunny soil sandy-loamy, chalky	Grey to white felted small panicles; has a highly filigreed effect that is good for mixing with other plants.
Cerastium tomentosum Snow-in-summer	10–15cm (4–6in)	late spring – early summer	white, small star shapes	sunny, warm soil permeable, sandy-loamy, barren, dry	Creates silver-grey carpets; covers the ground in dry places, walls, gaps between paving stones; attractive with low-growing bellflowers.
Echinops ritro, E. bannaticus Globe thistle	80–120cm (32–48in)	midsummer – early autumn	blue, ball shapes	sunny, warm soil permeable, dry, chalky	The flower heads remain decorative into the winter; suitable as solitary plants; attractive with *Achillea, Cephalaris* and *Lythrum*.
Eryngium alpinum Alpine eryngo	60–80cm (24–32in)	midsummer – late summer	steel blue with star-shaped upper leaves	sunny, warm soil dry, sandy-silty, chalky	Decorative fruits in winter; beautiful with *Gypsophila, Anaphilis, Solidago* and grasses such as *Molinia* and *Stipa*.

Name	Height	Flowering time	Flowers	Situation	Notes
Helichrysum italicum ssp. *serotinum* Curry plant	30–40cm (12–16in)	midsummer – late summer	sulphur-yellow	sunny, warm soil permeable, no water	Grey, leafy subshrub with closed shape; evergreen gap filler and mediator; protect against the wet in winter.
Helichrysum petiolare 'Silberwolke' or 'Silver' Liquorice plant	20–25cm (8–10in)	does not flower	none	sunny to partially shady soil rich in nutrients, with humus	Grey silvery foliage; as an annual ornamental leaved plant can enrich not only a balcony display.
Helichrysum 'Schweffellicht' Silver everlasting	25cm (10in)	midsummer – early autumn	sulphur-yellow (the pure species is sunny yellow)	sunny, warm soil permeable, silty, not too rich in nutrients	The grey leaves are woolly and white, compact growth; beautiful with *Origanum* 'Herrenhausen', *Sedum telephium, Nepeta*.
Lavandula angustifolia Lavender	30–60cm (12–24in)	summer	blue-violet heads	sunny, warm soil dry, permeable, chalky, silty	Evergreen grey subshrub; also white and pink varieties; combines well with most sunny herbaceous perennials; classic companion for roses.
Lychnis coronaria Rose campion	50cm (20in)	early summer – late summer	brilliant carmine	sunny soil permeable, with humus, not too moist	Herbaceous perennial with white-grey felted shoots and leaves; also white variety 'Alba'; beautiful with delphiniums, sage and Shasta daisies.
Nepeta x faassenii Catmint	20–60cm (8–24in)	early summer – early autumn	violet-blue panicles	sunny, warm soil permeable, dry, by no means heavy or wet	Grey-green shoots, pinch out half after the first flowers in July, this leads to compact growth; also white varieties; attractive plant for borders, walls, roses.
Perovskia atriplicifolia *Perovskia abrotanoides* Russian sage	70–120cm (28–48in)	late summer – early autumn	small violet, tubular, in tall panicles	sunny soil permeable, not wet	A herbaceous perennial that creates dense silver carpets of leaves; beautiful with Carpathian bellflowers and grasses such as *Helictotrichon* and *Festuca*.
Salvia argentea Silver sage	120cm (48in)	midsummer	white	sunny soil with humus, permeable, chalky	Very hairy silver-white leaves; short-lived and usually grown as a biennial herbaceous perennial; highly decorative accompanying plant.
Stachys byzantina Lamb's ears	30cm (12in)	midsummer – late summer	pale pink, unassuming	sunny, warm soil permeable, dry, low in nutrients	Silver woolly herbaceous perennial that creates carpet-like plantings; attractive in the foreground of borders and for walls and rockeries.
Veronica spicata ssp. *incana* Speedwell	20–40cm (8–16in)	summer	dark blue	sunny soil permeable, rather dry, low in nutrients	Silvery subshrub with tall filigree flowers; looks beautiful with cream and salmon-coloured roses; prune in the spring.

Glossary

accent plant - Any plant that is used to draw the eye in a bed or border or in a container. Accents might be created with tall plants in a mostly low-growing border or a spreading plant on an otherwise unadorned lawn.

annual - A plant that grows, flowers, produces seed and dies in one growing season - spring to autumn or winter. Some plants that cannot survive frosty weather without protection, such as canna lilies, are often grown as annuals and then discarded, even though they could survive for many more years.

architectural plant - A plant with a striking shape, such as a weeping tree, or an interesting leaf form, such as spiky or huge and glossy. Architectural plants are often used for accents.

bedding plant - Usually annuals, grown for their flowers or attractive foliage, bedding plants are used en masse to create a vivid but short-lived display. Although they are associated with large flowerbeds, such as those in municipal parks, they can be used successfully in private gardens, too. Common bedding plants are primulas and wallflowers in spring plantings and salvias and canna lilies in summer displays.

biennial - A plant that survives two years, growing in the first year and producing flowers and seeds in the following year before dying. Some plants, such as wallflowers, are grown as biennials, even though they are capable of living for longer.

bulb - A bulb is a storage organ, usually underground, from which a plant can grow. Bulbs are made up of numerous leaves or leaf-like structures wrapped around each other and getting smaller towards the bulb centre. Onions and daffodils are bulbs.

compost - vegetative material from the kitchen and garden that is rotted down and then used to improve the quality of all soils. A good compost heap is made of a mixture of coarse material, such as vegetable peelings and green stems, and finer material, such as grass clippings and seedling weeds. Good compost is virtually odourless or smells quite pleasant. Always mix grass clippings in well with other material to prevent them clumping together in a smelly mass.

corm - Like a bulb, a corm is a storage organ like a squashed fleshy stem from which a plant can grow. Cyclamen, crocuses and montbretia are corms.

crown - Herbaceous perennials die down to a crown and roots in the winter. The crown is the cluster of dormant buds at the soil surface that will produce the next year's plant.

cultivar - A cultivar is a plant that varies in some way from the species to which it is related, perhaps having bigger flowers or being smaller or larger in growth. 'Cultivar' is short for 'cultivated variety'; cultivars are usually plants that have been deliberately bred or selected in gardens or nurseries. For example, the cultivar *Salvia patens* 'Cambridge Blue' has pale blue flowers, whereas those of the species, *Salvia patens*, are rich dark blue.

evergreen - An evergreen plant is one that is never without leaves at any point in the year. Perennials, shrubs and trees can all be evergreen.

fleece - Thin horticultural sheeting used to protect seedlings and frost-vulnerable plants.

formal garden - Any garden that has a strong structure and repeated shapes. Formal gardens are usually kept extremely neat and tidy. Formality can be created with patterned layouts, such as knot gardens and parterres, clipped plant shapes, like box *(Buxus)* or other hedging, and strong architectural features, such as paths and walls, and so on.

framework - In a garden, the framework is the underlying structure, the evergreens, the deciduous trees and the paths and other features, that will be visible in some form all year round.

gazebo - From the Persian meaning a platform to view the moon, a gazebo is a an enclosed, roofed structure, such as a summerhouse, often circular or hexagonal, and usually intended for sitting beneath.

genus - A plant genus (for example *Geranium*) consists of a group of plants that share a number of characteristics, such as flower appearance, general leaf shape, root structure and so on. The plural form is genera.

graft - A graft is produced when a shoot or part of a shoot of one plant is joined to the roots of another. Grafts are common in fruit trees, such as apples, because they enable the breeder to ensure that a tree will grow strongly but be of a predictable size, such as dwarf or medium. Ornamentals, such as roses, may be grafted to produce a plant of a reasonable size more quickly than it would grow naturally on its own roots or to ensure that the plant grows more healthily than it would on its own roots.

herbaceous perennial - A non-woody plant that lives for two years or more, appearing from a rootstock in spring and dying down for winter.

humus - Well-rotted vegetative matter, such as leaf mould or garden compost, that bulks out the soil, increasing fertility and water retention.

hybrid - A hybrid plant occurs when two different plants are crossed, such as two species in the same genus or two species in different genera. Hybrids can occur in the wild but they are often the result of deliberate breeding to produce plants with improved characteristics to the naturally occuring forms.

informal garden - An informal garden is any garden that is not formal. Informal gardens can contain elements of formality, such as clipped hedges or straight-edged flowerbeds, but they usually lack any sort of uniformity and symmetry and are more free in their planting. Cottage gardens are generally informal.

mulch - A material used to cover bear soil to retain water and reduce weed growth. Mulches can be bark, compost, gravel, black plastic and so on.

marginal plant - Marginal plants are so named because their preferred growing conditions - moist or wet soil - are found on the margins of ponds and other water sources.

naturalize - Some plants, such as species daffodils, primroses and cyclamen, are wonderful for naturalizing, which means that they can be planted in areas where the soil is not usually cultivated, such as in grass, under trees or on banks, and allowed to spread more or less unchecked.

panorama - A wide, open view seen from one point.

parterre - A garden with formally arranged geometrical flowerbeds.

pergola - A rectangular or square garden structure consisting of an equal number of upright supports bearing long beams and a series of crossbeams. The structure creates a lightly shaded area or walkway and is often used as a support for climbing plants such as roses and clematis.

pleach - To intertwine branches, especially when making a hedge. With pleached avenues the lower branches are often also removed.

rhizome - A fleshy stem-like underground organ from which a plant can grow. Rhizomes often grow horizontally and are one of the means by which a plant spreads. Irises have rhizomes that often grow on the soil surface.

rill - A very thin stretch of water, often moving, as in a small brook. Ornamental rills, with straight, stone-line banks, are often found in formal gardens.

rootstock - This can refer to the roots of any plant but more usually is used to refer to the roots and crown of herbaceous perennials and the roots that are used in grafting.

soil pH - Some plants are very sensitive to the acidity or alkalinity of the soil, which is measured in a scale from pH1, very acid, to pH14, very alkaline; pH7 is neutral. Plants such as camellias and rhododendrons require an acid soil to grow well.

species - In each genus there is one or more species (for example *Geranium endressii*). These are individual plants that share all the same characteristics. Unlike a cultivar, a species is a distinct plant that has evolved in the wild and all its offspring look the same.

subspecies (ssp.) - These are plants within a species that vary in some way from what is regarded as the true type. They might be identical to the species but have hairier leaves, for example.

topiary - Trimming and training plants, such as box (*Buxus*) and yew (*Taxus*), into geometric and representative shapes, including orbs, spirals, pyramids, birds and animals. The trimmed plants themselves are also called topiary.

tuber - Like a bulb, a tuber is a storage organ, usually underground, from which a plant can grow. Potatoes and dahlias are tubers.

vista - In gardens, vistas are usually a view glimpsed at the end of a long narrow opening, such as an avenue of yew hedging with a statue or other focal point at the end.